SCRAP QUILTS
and How to Make Them

Judy Florence

Dover Publications, Inc.
New York

To my son Matt.

This new edition is also dedicated
to the memory of my friend and
photographer, Jim Christoffersen,
1938–1992.

Other Books by the Author

Award-Winning Quilts and How to Make Them
Award-Winning Quilts and How to Make Them, Book II
Award-Winning Quick Quilts
A Collection of Favorite Quilts: Narratives, Directions & Patterns for 15 Quilts
More Projects & Patterns: A Second Collection of Favorite Quilts

Interior layout: Janice Fary
Editor: Tammie Taylor
Photographs: Jim Christoffersen

Bibliographical Note

This Dover edition, first published in 1995, is a slightly altered republication of *Award-Winning Scrap
Quilts*, originally published by Wallace-Homestead Book Company, Radnor, Pennsylvania, in 1987. Four
additional photographs of quilt details—"Bowtie," "Brickwork," "Alphabetical by Flavor" and "Attic
Windows"—have been added to the color section. Four blank pages have been removed from the front of the
Book; the book now begins with page 5.

Library of Congress Cataloging-in-Publication Data

Florence, Judy.
    Scrap quilts and how to make them / Judy Florence.
        p.   cm.
    Rev. ed. of: Award-winning quilts. Radnor, Penn. : Wallace-Homestead Book Co., 1987.
    Includes bibliographical references.
    ISBN 0-486-28477-8
    1. Patchwork—Patterns. 2. Quilting—Patterns. 3. Quilts. I. Florence, Judy. Award-winning
scrap quilts.   II. Title.
TT835.F623   1995
746.46—dc20   94-40102
                                                                                                    CIP

Manufactured in the United States of America
Dover Publications, Inc., 31 East 2nd Street, Mineola, N.Y. 11501

Contents

Preface

What is it about scrap quilts that is so compelling? Each scrap quilt has a distinct charm of its own, like the very fabrics from which it is made. Each is a reflection of the tremendous variety in the tastes of quiltmakers.

Quiltmakers appear to have come full circle. They now recognize the beauty and freedom expressed in early scrap quilts. Contemporary quilt designers are using fabric mixtures to regain that freedom and vitality. These new designs are reminiscent of the "scrap-bag" quilts, in an elegant and contemporary way.

Scrap quilts are practical and economical to make. Designers of scrap quilts are able to make something out of a modest collection of fabrics. They are able to blend a medley of fabrics and colors to produce a design that captivates the maker, the viewer, and the collector alike.

In scrap quilt design, there are few restrictions or regulations by which to abide. This leaves plenty of room for imagination and greater latitude for exploring patterns and designs beyond the traditional. You can lay aside the barriers and blinders associated with conventional patterns—relinquish the rules that frequently stifle quilt design.

As this book makes clear, successful scrap quilts are notably fundamental. Simple patterns combined with a certain measure of attention to clever detail result in an intriguing scrap design. A suitable pattern, careful selection and placement of fabrics, and excellent workmanship spell the difference between an ordinary scrap quilt and an outstanding one.

Above all, making scrap quilts is fun and relaxing. You are free to experiment with fabrics with a sense of abandon, free to use your design as a "playground" for mixtures. Ideas, colors, and designs mingle together in unforeseen ways. Expect to derive a great deal of satisfaction in designing a quilt with the special fabrics in your collection.

Acknowledgments

Some of the quilts included in this book were created by special Eau Claire quilting friends. Thanks to Alice Weickelt for her Hole in the Barn Door quilt, which she designed, pieced, and quilted. Thanks to Mary Mousel for sharing her Escape, a quilt which represents a culmination of her years of home decorating, flower arranging, and quilting. And thanks to the Tuesday Quilters of Eau Claire for their assistance with the Bow Tie featured in this book.

I would also like to thank several special people for graciously donating fabric needed for the Alphabetical by Flavor quilt: Dorothy Gilbertson, Marie Halmstad, Gloria Linnell, Mary Mousel, Ann Ohl, Eilene Paulson, and Pat Simonsen.

Part 1
Building Your Perspective

1
How to Use This Book

This book is divided into two main sections. The first part includes general information for the prospective scrap-quilt designer. The second part includes specific instructions for making seven impressive scrap quilts.

Where to Begin

In the next five chapters, you will find a helpful base of information to consider as you begin your scrap quilt. There are tips on organizing your fabric collection, ideas for getting started with your design, descriptions of available patterns, and pointers on adapting traditional designs to make your scrap quilt unique. Diagrams accompanying the discussion make it easier for you to compare alternatives and to identify subtleties that can only be suggested in text.

In addition, the resources listed in Chapter 6 provide quite a variety of colorful references to study as you decide which quilt best suits you and your scrap collection. A pattern sketch of each quilt is included so you can limit your search to possibilities that definitely interest you.

Getting Organized

The second part of the book includes a detailed supply list, full-sized patterns, and complete directions for the cutting, assembly, and finishing of each of seven quilts. Diagrams speed the quilt-ing process along, and color photos provide still more detail—as well as incentive for finishing what promises to be a beautiful piece of handiwork.

You'll also appreciate the suggested design variations included in each set of instructions, especially if you're new to scrap quilting. These alternatives help you adhere to a proven design as you transform your assortment of fabrics into a quilt that is nevertheless quite original.

Experience Preferred?

Difficulty levels range from elementary to moderately difficult. The Attic Windows wall hanging features large pieces with simple design and construction methods. The Stars and Bars quilt calls for intricate piecing and careful selection and placement of plaid fabrics. The other five quilts fall somewhere in between, with varied levels of skill and design required.

The instructional material throughout the book assumes a general knowledge of quilting techniques. For more of the basics in quiltmaking, refer to my previous books, *Award-Winning Quilts and How To Make Them* and *Award-Winning Quilts, Book II*.

2
Managing Your Fabric

Building Your Fabric Collection

Many quiltmakers already have a sufficient or abundant supply of fabric. That may be the reason you picked up this book in the first place—perhaps you are looking for a way to reduce your collection.

Other quiltmakers have taken up quilting recently and have a limited mixture and volume of fabric. They may be looking for hints on how to build a satisfactory and workable collection.

Most quiltmakers, however, are continually building and depleting their fabric stores. They use up fabrics at a fairly steady rate. They add to their collection at a somewhat faster rate, in an attempt to keep a substantial variety at their disposal.

Building and maintaining your fabric assortment doesn't have to be a major project. On the other hand, you won't regret giving it some careful thought. Here are some suggestions to help you:

• First, take inventory. Determine what scraps and fabrics you already have on hand.
• Next, determine what colors or types of fabrics you need to add to make a workable collection.
• Then, actively add to your collection.

Much of your fabric probably has been neglected. Some of it hasn't been looked at or used in years. Look through it now. You may be pleasantly surprised at the variety you find. What you thought was unsuitable a few years ago may be all the rage in quilting now.

Accomplished quilters and designers agree that the key to a workable fabric collection is wide variety. In *The Complete Book of Quiltmaking*, Michele Walker suggests, "Make a wide-ranging fabric collection, something between a colour palette and a scrap-bag. Above all, avoid buying sets of ready-assorted fabrics for patchwork, a practice equivalent to painting by number."

In fact, the amount of variety in the collection determines your success with fabric mixtures. Too much similarity in fabrics is monotonous; designs become predictable, passive, and—in some cases— even boring. Roberta Horton's *Calico and Beyond* warns, "If everything is too similar, your eyes won't spend the time to examine each part; they will just skim over the whole. Remember, the idea is to keep the viewers' attention; you can accomplish this by making their eyes linger on the fabric."

How do quiltmakers add to their collections? There are many sources. One of my friends has a theory regarding scraps: "If you set a box of scraps in a dark corner, they will keep multiplying!" This may be true. Even so, I think you can have a little more control over the building of your fabric collection, even if it only means deciding which scraps to set in the dark corner.

Serious quilters have found other ways to build their collection. *Scrap Quilts'* author Judy Martin devotes an entire chapter to methods of collecting fabrics for scrap quilts. It is packed with good ideas ranging from "Swap with friends" to "Tell your relatives who travel that you're collecting fabrics. They'll have an easy time shopping for souvenirs for you."

Consider fabric exchanges. Let people know that you are interested in fabrics. You may soon have more than you anticipated.

Over the years, I have had many offers for scraps and fabrics that others were discarding. There have been so many offers, in fact, that I have to be careful that I don't accept more than I can find a place for.

Recently, for instance, a friend offered me her substantial accumulation of fabrics. She had taken some quilting classes and decided that it was not for her. Plus, she was disposing of all her fabrics from home sewing (as well as quilting) projects. She guessed she had 10 to 20 garbage bags full. She was cleaning the attic of her large country home, had taken three trailer loads of "stuff" to the dump, and the next load was going to be the fabric. Did I want it?

Because I knew her collection would include many suitable quilt fabrics, I was reluctant to reject her generous offer. But I knew I didn't have the time, space, or inclination to sort through and store so much fabric—fabric that I had not even seen.

If I accepted all the old quilts and scrap fabrics offered to me, they would take up the space of a car in our garage. I have accepted many quilts and fabrics, only to decide later that they were not useful to me in any way. I have since learned to accept such offers provided that the giver understands that I'll use the fabric as it best suits my needs. I have learned not to be afraid to say, "Yes, thank you; I will gladly take it and keep what I can use, then offer the rest to quilting friends, Goodwill, or anyone else who can use it." I have also learned that there are times when it's best to say, "No, thank you; my supply is adequate right now," or "Thanks, but I just don't have enough storage space."

When my friend with the "ten bags full" made her offer, I recruited another friend who was sure to be interested in this offer (she was making a charm quilt). We set up a streamlined sorting system, reserving and dividing the fabrics that were of interest to us and passing on lots of fabric to another friend who makes quilts from all types of material.

That way, at least four people benefited from the offer. I added some unusual new-to-me fabrics to my collection. My friend received dozens of additional swatches for her 999-fabric charm quilt. Another quilter received yards of fabric for her functional family quilts. And the first woman got her attic cleaned out.

There is little agreement on how much fabric to buy when you're purchasing new yardage for your collection. Opinion runs from "Never buy less than three yards of anything, just in case you want it for the border of a queen-size quilt" to "Buy only small pieces, about one-half yard, so

you won't grow tired of the fabric from seeing too much of it." Roberta Horton suggests, "Buying only a little bit of fabric also means the excitement of running out." I tend to like that idea.

Add colors and fabrics that you don't ordinarily use. These will be invaluable in fabric mixture designs. Michele Walker comments, "In order for a design's potential to be fully realized . . . you may have to incorporate colours you would not normally have thought of using; some bright complementary focal point to set off a moody area of muted tones, for example, or a patterned fabric to texture a particular shape or area."

You may find the section called "Ideas for Sorting and Storing" (below) helpful as you evaluate your fabric collection. It includes a list of several types of fabrics that are popular for scrap quilting.

Preparing Your Fabric Collection

It is smart to prepare and store your fabrics so they are ready for use at any time. Rather than wondering at some later time if a particular scrap has been washed, do it when you acquire the fabric. This will eliminate any doubt and save time in the end. Here are some recommendations for preparing your fabrics:

Wash all fabrics. Three good reasons for washing are to ascertain colorfastness, to eliminate any potential shrinkage problems, and to remove soil or odor from fabrics that have been in storage for an extended time.

To wash larger pieces or amounts, use warm water and mild soap in the washing machine. Let the fabrics soak for a few minutes, especially if the fabric is soiled or has an odor from improper care or prolonged storage. Then wash the fabric for just a couple minutes on the gentle or delicate cycle to prevent excessive raveling. Rinse thoroughly, and spin to remove excess moisture.

Smaller fabric pieces may be washed by hand. If you are certain of their colorfastness, several scraps can be laundered together in the machine. If you are uncertain about the colorfastness of any fabric, wash the item separately. If it is *not* colorfast, continue to wash it in hot water until the color no longer runs.

Dry fabrics with care. Select a gentle or delicate cycle on the dryer, using warm air (not hot) or "air only," until fabrics are damp-dry. Or you may drape fabrics over a wooden clothes rack or clothesline.

Press all fabrics. This is easier to do while they are still damp-dry (especially with 100-percent cotton).

Trim fabric to remove raveled edges. Also trim misshapen pieces, removing odds and ends that are not useful.

Ideas for Sorting and Storing

From one quiltmaker to the next, the amount of fabric (and of space that can be devoted to storing it) in each collection varies widely. Some quiltmakers have just the beginning of a collection of appropriate fabrics. Others have shelves, closets, trunks, or rooms full of fabric. Some are working with scraps from previous clothing projects, cuttings from garment fabrics, or gleanings from a secondhand store. Others have hundreds (or thousands) of dollars' worth of fabric, one yard minimum, in every color sequence.

Sorting and storage needs, then, will vary just as widely. But whether you can get by with just a shoebox or need a computer to keep track of your fabric, you might consider the following ideas.

Store fabrics neatly for easy viewing and selection. So that color, texture, and design are obvious, fold fabrics into piles with right sides out. Store in containers of your choice. If you use clear containers, be sure that they are not exposed to direct sunlight or bright lights. Containers that block out light will help to preserve the colors in your fabrics. This may not be convenient when you're searching for specific fabrics, but if you're concerned about maintaining your original colors, it's worthwhile to use more protective containers for storage. Perhaps you can develop a system for labeling them to solve the problem of quickly identifying their contents.

Arrange fabrics according to color. Many quilters like to store fabrics by color group. They stack or group fabrics in a rainbow array. If you do this, consider separating the print fabrics from the solid colors. Then you won't have to interrupt the design process to go rummaging through every color group should you decide to work only in prints or only in solids.

Storage by color is also best if you tend to design around a color theme. (See Chapter 4, "Five Design Approaches for Scrap Quilts.")

Organize your collection by fabric type. Fabrics may be stored by groups depending on the nature and size of their design. Examples of some groups include

- Solids
- Microdots and pin-dots
- Fine prints (overall)
- Medium prints (overall)
- Bold prints (overall)
- Border prints
- Stripes
- Plaids
- Challenging or exotic fabrics
- Prints with white background
- Questionable fabrics
- Miscellaneous

Some quiltmakers prefer storage by type of fabric because they tend to design by type of fabric, as well (see Chapter 4).

Building a Workable Resource File

Of course your fabric collection is the most important resource in planning a scrap quilt. But you will also enjoy drawing from other resources. A file of references, ideas, sketches, and clippings will be an invaluable aid as you consider all the possibilities for your quilt design. The next chapter, "Types of Scrap Quilt Designs," offers an excellent starting point for organizing such a file.

3
Types of Scrap Quilt Designs

Throughout this discussion of types of scrap designs, try to have several pictures of fabric-mixture quilts at hand. These may be magazine clippings, quilt books and periodicals, or the color plates from engagement calendars that feature quilts as illustrations. Collect any clippings you can find in a notebook or pocket folder (and include a few sheets of graph paper so you'll be able to sketch the patterns you're interested in using and adapting). As you read the description for each type of scrap quilt, try to find examples in your file of the traditional patterns mentioned, and list the ones you like.

Know the Options

By definition, all scrap quilts differ from each other. Therein lies their appeal. However, if you look closely at the way scrap quilts are put together, you'll see some similarities. Recognition of these similarities is helpful in determining why one scrap quilt design may be more effective than another. In addition, knowing the types of designs available will give you a good variety of ideas for making your own successful quilts.

The following groups are based mainly on construction and the effect of primary and secondary designs. The grouping is frequently dependent on the *set* of the design—that is, how the units are placed in relation to one another or in relation to latticework or borders.

The groups outlined here are not sacredly defined or separated. There may be overlap between groups, and some scrap quilt designs may fit into more than one class. You may discover additional groups to add to the list.

Five Popular Groups

Separate block

When people hear the words *scrap quilt*, it is not unusual for them to picture traditional patterns like Dresden Plates, Pinwheels, and Log Cabins. These are often set block-to-block or with an alternate plain block, using numerous colorful, small prints against a light, solid background.

Separate block designs are the most widely recognized scrap quilts. They are also the most elementary to plan and construct. Many traditional block patterns are easily adapted for scrap use. In fact, that's probably how most traditional patterns were first made—with scrap mixtures.

In addition to the more familiar block patterns, there are several less frequently used patterns that are perfect candidates for scrap design. One example is the Album block and its variations. The basic Album unit is flexible enough to allow for the use of many fabrics, a choice of four-patch or nine-patch blocks, and a choice of horizontal or diamond set. Excellent examples of Album scrap quilts based on separate-block placement are found in the book *Remember Me* (see the Bibliography).

Separate-block scrap designs may also feature appliqués. The popular heart motif is ideal for scraps. A mixture of fabrics—bold prints, plaids, microdots, solids—can be combined in one harmonious statement, each appliqué in a different fabric, but all unified by their common shape.

Overall design

Some quilts feature patterns and pieces that flow together for a total statement, a design that includes everything on the quilt surface at once. These quilts have an *overall* effect—you're impressed by their total design, and don't focus on the separate units.

A prime example of an overall scrap design is the Tumbling Blocks and its variations. Each fabric piece works with all of its neighboring pieces to create a design that moves throughout the surface, unbounded by any unit or block restrictions.

Quilts that use the Tumbling Block diamond or the equilateral triangle usually result in overall designs. The mere number of pieces required (usually several hundred) to complete one of these quilts insures plenty of territory to work in all sorts of fabrics. The blending of so many fabrics creates an impressive overall design.

Secondary design

Many scrap quilt patterns contain pieces that react with neighboring units or latticework to create *secondary* patterns. These secondary patterns come as a surprise, and usually a welcome one, at that. Scrap quilts with secondary designs are visually more interesting. The interplay between shapes and patterns often adds a note of vitality and excitement to the design.

Most quiltmakers are familiar with the secondary designs of the Log Cabin. Basic blocks, simply divided diagonally into light and dark halves, can be arranged in countless ways to form secondary designs such as Barn-Raising, Straight Furrow, and so on. This process works with a number of other patterns, as well. Simple geometric designs set flush with each other, or strategically placed against a pieced latticework, can result in impressive secondary designs, some which may even dominate over the intended primary design.

Half-a-Square triangles (see Diagram 1) lend themselves well to secondary designs. A light and a dark triangle can be pieced to form a unit that divides diagonally into half light and half dark. These can, in turn, be arranged into larger units, as in Diagram 2. Imagine the designs that could result from setting several of these larger units adjacent to one another.

Like the Log Cabin, the basic nine-patch combination of squares and triangles (Diagram 3) can be used in quite a variety of arrangements. This very fundamental scrap unit can produce dramatic secondary designs such as the one featured in Diagram 4.

Another familiar pattern with graphic secondary design is Ocean Waves. The basic unit is shown in Diagram 5; it may include scraps and a unifying background color. As each unit is placed adjacent to the next, a network of prominent diamond paths begins to form, as in Diagram 6. In the end, this secondary design becomes the primary design, the original Ocean Wave units becoming barely distinguishable. Many quiltmakers have a difficult time identifying the Ocean Waves primary construction unit since its secondary effect is so strong.

Diagram 1. Half-a-Square Triangle

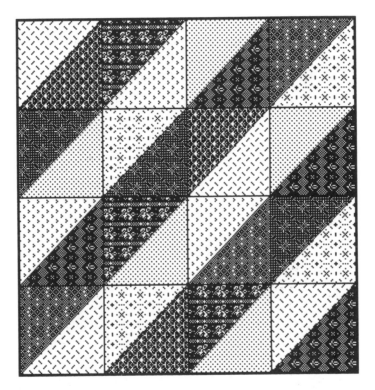

Diagram 2. Combined Half-a-Square Triangle Units

Secondary designs can also be formed by the combination of two traditional blocks. When placed adjacent to one another, the conventional patterns often take on a fresh look. Many scrap quilts incorporate two traditional patterns, such as the Star and the Log Cabin, or the Kaleidoscope and a nine-patch. The resulting images are usually more appealing and more complex—prime ground for fabric mixtures.

Combining two patterns is a painless way to come up with an original quilt design. Special patterns and articles featuring the combination of two blocks have been increasingly popular in recent quilt books and periodicals.

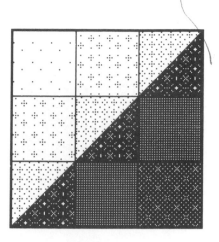

Diagram 3. Nine-Patch

Diagram 4. Nine-Patch Units Combined in
Zigzag Layout

Several of the quilts featured in this book form secondary designs: Attic Windows creates a diagonal straight-furrow design; Stars and Bars creates a Japanese lantern and vertical bar effect; and the Bow Tie forms a transparent gridwork of dark octagons. Take a moment to look at the photographs and find the secondary designs.

Curved-piece illusion

In *curved-piece illusion* designs, the geometric lines progress gradually to form hexagons, octagons, and larger polygons that appear somewhat rounded. This illusion of curved piecing is often pronounced.

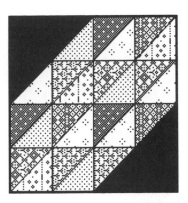

Diagram 5. Ocean Waves (Basic Unit)

Diagram 6. Ocean Waves Combined Units

Curved-piece illusion designs are especially effective when done in scraps. The mixture and blend of so many fabrics and textures contributes to the lines' gradual flow from piece to piece, the quality that gives them the look of curves. So the success of the curved illusion depends on the use of a broad mixture of fabrics in contrasting shades to make the illusion even more subtle and effective.

Two well-known patterns with graphic curved illusions are Kaleidoscope and Storm at Sea. Both are excellent candidates for fabric mixtures and have frequently been executed in scraps. Their linear shapes sometimes take on unexpected characteristics, but the result is almost always pleasing.

21

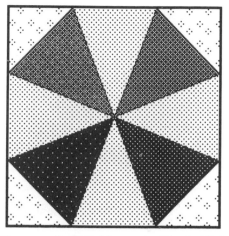

Diagram 7. Kaleidoscope (Basic Unit)

Diagram 8. Kaleidoscope Combined Units

In particular, the Kaleidoscope and its variations have been explored in recent periodicals and books. Kaleidoscope (Diagram 7) offers good opportunity for exploring design possibilities. For instance, it has great scrap potential for placement of light and dark fabrics to create stately stars and gentle curves. Diagram 8 gives a hint of the illusion of curves created by adjacent pieces in Kaleidoscope.

By itself, the Storm at Sea unit is fairly static (see Diagram 9), though it gives more of an impression of curves than the individual Kaleidoscope unit does. When joined together in their traditional pieced latticework, however, Storm at Sea units create a wavy pattern: an impression of intertwining circles that swirl and tumble across the quilt surface.

22

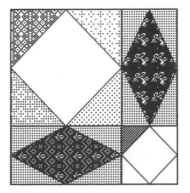

Diagram 9. Storm at Sea (Basic Unit)

Diagram 10. Storm at Sea Combined Units

See Chapter 6, "Some Traditional Patterns Suitable for Scrap Quilts," for a list of references that picture Kaleidoscope and Storm at Sea designs.

Charm quilts

Scraps and the charm concept naturally go hand-in-hand. In a *charm* quilt, no two pieces are cut from the same fabric. Although many charm quilts are planned for their design effect, some are purely collections of pieces from a lot of different fabrics, each cut in the same shape, assembled into one fascinating composition. The Alphabetical by Flavor quilt included in Part 2 of this book fits the definition of a charm quilt. No fabrics were repeated; only one shape was used; and friends contributed a variety of fabrics.

An outstanding reference on the history and technique of charm quilts is Beyer's *The Scrap Look* (see the Bibliography).

Updating Your Scrap Book

Don't abandon the file suggested earlier when you've finished reading this chapter; it will prove to be an excellent resource whenever you work on new designs. It's even a good idea to include a bibliography in the file as you discover good books and magazines about fabric-mixture quilts. (Begin with some from the Bibliography at the end of this book.) Go a step further and make a list of pictures of outstanding scrap quilts, by book or magazine title and page number. Once you are familiar with the types of scrap quilts, you'll begin to recognize unusual ideas that can be incorporated into good-looking scrap designs, and your resource file is the perfect place for keeping track of those ideas.

4
Five Design Approaches for Scrap Quilts

Plan for Success

Successful fabric-mixture quilt designs don't just happen; some planning is essential. The starting place is not always easy to find. In fact, the starting point may be at an entirely different place for each quiltmaker and each quilt.

I have approached and taught scrap quilt design from several vantage points, and different students have found success with each of these methods. So I'm suggesting these design approaches as ideas on where to begin. Each approach has some necessary boundaries and guidelines to help you set reasonably challenging goals for your scrap quilt project.

Consider the Possibilities

You may select one approach or combine a couple of approaches in your design. Each discussion includes examples of how the approach was used in the quilts featured in Part 2.

Select a color theme. You could choose to begin with a specific color theme of your preference. Sort through (or recall) your fabric collection and consider the colors or range of colors in which you would like to work. It may be any kind of color or color theme. When you've decided, dig into your fabrics and find all the examples that fit into that color scheme.

Example: Look at the color photograph of Mary Mousel's Escape ('Round the Twist variation) quilt. Mary's accumulation of fabric was substantial—the result of several years of designing and making custom draperies, clothes, and quilts—which basically gave her the freedom to use whatever color she wanted.

She chose a burgundy color range. Then she gathered all the related fabrics she could find in her collection. A fabric was considered acceptable as long as it contained a hint of burgundy or rose and did not clash with the other fabrics. This included fine prints, bold prints, border prints, and stripes. Mary combined the patterned scraps with deep wine and rose solids. The resulting Escape is said to be *monochromatic*, since it concentrates on a single color area. The success of the design is due to Mary's mixture of many scrap fabrics and her thoughtful placement of the light and dark solids.

Select a basic shape. If just looking through the variety and colors of your fabric collection staggers you, then you might begin with a basic pattern shape. Forget your fabrics for a while and concentrate on a shape. Select a simple one, such as a rectangle, square, or triangle. Other quadrilaterals, polygons, and tessellated (mosaic-type) shapes are good possibilities. One-patch and two-patch shapes also make appropriate starting points. Look through Chapter 6, "Some Traditional Patterns Suitable for Scrap Quilts," for ideas.

Example: Look at the color photograph of the Brickwork quilt. Its maker had little else in mind when Brickwork was in its early design stages except the basic *shape*—a rectangle. The selection of such an ordinary shape opened wide the possibilities for using a large assortment of fabrics.

In fact, the Brickwork pattern has almost no limits on fabric usage: The designer has only to designate fabrics as light or dark. Nearly all fabrics, whatever color, type of print, or degree of lightness and darkness, would be appropriate. It's an excellent example of how selecting one basic shape makes the fabric decisions much easier.

Select a type of fabric. You may have an inclination to work with a specific type or group of fabrics, such as border prints, bold prints, solids, plaids, stripes, and so on. If so, begin by choosing the type you prefer among those available in your fabric collection. This is not to say that you must confine yourself to only one type of fabric. Rather, select one as your starting point. Then expand into more fabrics as you develop your design.

Example: Look at the color photograph of the Stars and Bars quilt. This one is a result of my interest in incorporating plaid fabrics into quilt designs. My starting point was a box of plaid fabrics that had too long been ignored and pushed to the rear of the closet.

Sorting through the box, I eliminated any fabrics that created jarring contrasts. Next, I moved on to decisions about which fabrics would best complement the plaids, and which pattern would work well with them.

The final product, Stars and Bars, is a fairly complex quilt, but it began simply, with the inspiration of a growing pile of unused plaids.

Select a pattern. Perhaps there's a specific pattern you've been longing to make. Now is the time to pull it out of your file, draw it up, and work out a design in scrap fabrics.

You don't have to use an intricate pattern. On the contrary, a simple pattern is better (as is a simple shape), due to the variety and complexity of fabric mixtures that may be included in a simple design.

Many patterns are suitable for fabric mixtures: the Tumbling Blocks and its variations, Ocean Waves, Snail's Trail, and various four- and nine-patch patterns. Experienced quiltmakers could select more intricate patterns such as Kaleidoscope, Spider Web, or Storm at Sea, which lend themselves well to fabric mixtures.

Examples of the Bow Tie, Attic Windows, and Hole in the Barn Door are included in Part 2 of this book. Other suitable patterns are included in Chapter 6, "Some Traditional Patterns Suitable for Scrap Quilts."

Example: Look at the color photograph of the Hole in the Barn Door quilt. Alice Weickelt made this quilt for a friend for whom the pattern name had special meaning. Since the name of the pattern was of prime importance, this was Alice's starting point. She began with the Hole in the Barn Door pattern, a fairly elementary nine-patch design, and proceeded to design an impressive, colorful gradation of fabric scraps and mixtures.

Select an idea. You might begin a scrap quilt centered around a particular idea that is entirely unrelated to a pattern, color, or fabric. The idea may be as simple as a picture or graphic that you have seen. It may be an event or a memory. It may be some arbitrary (but practical) goal such as trying to use up all the fabric in the box on the top shelf on the left, or designing and making a queen-size quilt using six-inch squares without purchasing additional fabric. It may be a significant goal, such as designing a quilt using all the fabrics, and only the fabrics, used in your previous quilts, or designing a quilt with fabrics collected from your childhood friends. Any idea you have is worthy of consideration.

Example: Look at the color photograph of Alphabetical by Flavor. The design for this quilt was sparked by a colorful little brochure advertising jelly beans. I picked up the advertisement in a candy store. The orderly arrangement of the tasty, colorful jelly beans lined up and labeled in rows and columns immediately brought visions of carefully arranged fabrics to my mind.

I proceeded to gather 100-percent cotton solids of every color in my fabric collection. When I realized I didn't have nearly enough colors to represent all the flavors I was considering, I solicited additional fabrics from several friends. Then the fun began—assigning flavors to colors, and sorting and arranging fabrics like jelly beans in an advertisement.

What at first seemed like a silly idea grew into a lighthearted design that was great fun in the making. The starting point was the *idea*—rows of colorful jelly beans.

Don't dismiss any idea as a possibility for scrap quilt design, at least not right away.

Take Your Pick

It is not unusual to be overwhelmed by your fabric collection. What most quiltmakers need is a point in the right direction and a gentle nudge. Perhaps the five design approaches outlined above have done some pointing and nudging that you can appreciate. If you are feeling apprehensive about beginning such a project, just select one of these approaches, and you'll be on your way to creating an unprecedented scrap quilt.

5
Suggestions for Adapting Traditional Patterns

One of the best things about scrap quilts is that many successful ones are constructed from quite elementary traditional patterns. One-patch designs are perfect candidates for fabric mixtures. Rectangles, squares, triangles, and hexagons are one-patch shapes that are very adaptable to scraps.

Simple block patterns that contain only a few pieces also work well. Patterns with only two, three, four, or five pieces can be used successfully. Attic Windows and Bow Tie are prime examples of simple patterns (only three and five pieces, respectively) that lend themselves well to fabric mixtures.

In addition, because of their simplicity, both Attic Windows and Bow Tie can be arranged in numerous design variations and layouts. The way a simple scrap pattern is *set*—that is, how it is placed in relation to other blocks, alternate squares, latticework, or borders—is often the key to dramatic fabric-mixture designs. The following examples show some effects you can create with a variety of settings for Attic Windows and Bow Tie.

Attic Windows

First of all, consider the pattern shapes in Attic Windows (Diagram 1). There are only two shapes—the square and the trapezoid. The complete unit contains one square and two trapezoids. These three pieces provide options for three color variations in fabric—perhaps a dark scrap, a light scrap, and a solid.

A light scrap and a dark scrap are all you need to create interesting two-dimensional designs. The third fabric, perhaps a solid or otherwise uniform fabric, serves two functions: It helps unify the design, and it gives the three-dimensional

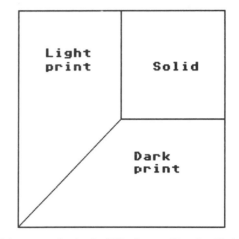

Diagram 1. Attic Windows (Basic Unit)

feeling to Attic Windows, the feeling of looking out a window, across a room, or from an attic. With strategic placement, you can create other "views": through a latticework or fence, or into another space—a garden, for instance.

Traditional. Diagram 2 features a traditional Attic Windows setting. All the dark-patterned fabric scraps are placed on the bottom of each unit. The light fabric scraps are placed on the left of each unit. A solid fabric is placed in the upper right-hand area. The sensation for most viewers is one of looking at a receding dark wall or window, with a light wall on the left and a dark floor in front.

By simply turning the page (Diagram 2) ninety degrees, you create different illusions. For instance, a ninety-degree turn to the right gives the sensation of a light-colored ceiling, a dark wall on the left, and a very dark wall or window at the rear. If you turn the diagram upside down, the

29

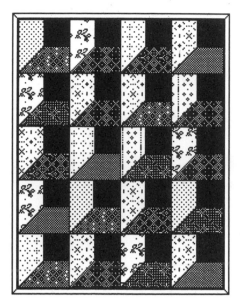

Diagram 2. Traditional Attic Windows Setting

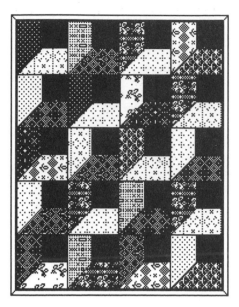

Diagram 3. Straight Furrow Setting for Attic Windows

ceiling appears dark, the right wall is light, and the far wall or window is completely dark. And so the design illusions change with each turn of the page.

Straight Furrow. The Attic Windows unit can be visually divided into two parts along the diagonal axis. Half of the unit is predominantly light; the other half, predominantly dark. In this respect, it is visually similar to the traditional Log Cabin block. It follows that any of the many Log Cabin variations are also possible with Attic Windows. The Straight Furrow variation in Diagram 3 is an example. Looking at this setting, you can imagine rays of light beaming diagonally from right to left. Or you may notice the dark "ribbons" running in the same direction.

Other Log Cabin variations can be achieved by rearranging the units. Because the diagonal light/dark division of Attic Windows is not as precise or rigid as the Log Cabin division, Attic Windows can be used in more subtle ways, with effects and lines that are less abrupt, more gentle.

Many other designs are possible. With a working palette of only 20 or 24 six-inch blocks, you can create innovative designs such as those in Diagrams 4 through 7. By simple rearrangement of the units, you can make new shapes and images appear.

Chevron. When you place a mirror image under the top half of Attic Windows, a row of chevrons forms across the center of the quilt. This Chevron variation (Diagram 4) might be compared to Barn-Raising. Imagine a mirror image of the entire design off to the right.

Skyscraper. The Skyscraper variation in Diagram 5 is formed by repeating a two-row unit that joins the dark squares in checkerboard fashion.

Japanese Lantern. Arranging four Attic Windows units so that the dark squares meet, two at the top center and two at the bottom center, generates a row of complete Japanese lanterns down the center of the quilt. Each half of the row is duplicated (on each side of the quilt) to form side borders of half-lanterns, which could have a sort of three-dimensional impact, depending on the colors used.

Broken Spools. The Broken Spools variation in Diagram 7 is a random layout. I simply laid down the twenty pieces—using the order they were in when I picked them up—with little regard for direction or placement. Several images of incomplete or broken-looking spools dominated the resulting design.

30

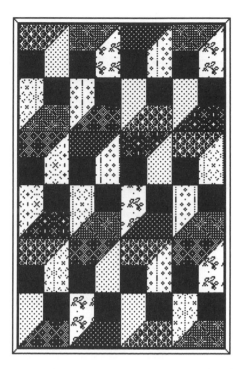

Diagram 4. Chevron Variation for Attic Windows

Diagram 5. Skyscraper Variation for Attic Windows

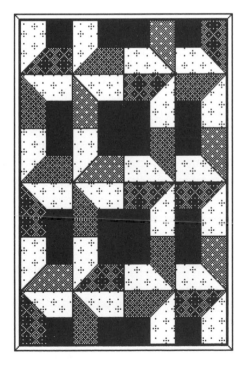

Diagram 7. Broken Spools Variation for Attic Windows

Diagram 6. Japanese Lantern Variation for Attic Windows

These are only six of numerous layout possibilities. Use these as a starting point and then go ahead and try your own Attic Windows designs. You can experiment freely by coloring in a grid. Make a copy of Diagram 8 or draw a similar grid on graph paper or plain white paper. Pencil in light- and dark-scrap trapezoids and dark solid squares. Then cut the paper into twenty units. Lay them on white or black paper in five rows. Arrange them in a design of your choice, and tape or glue them in place when you find a design that you really like. In addition to a layout that is uniquely yours, you will have a completed piece in fabric mixtures that is not likely to be duplicated.

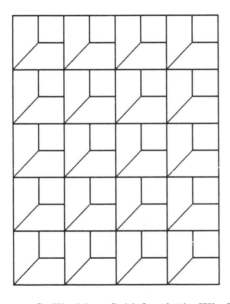

Diagram 8. Working Grid for Attic Windows

When I make an Attic Windows design, I usually cut all the fabric pieces first, making sure to cut several extras. Then I lay them on a large working surface and arrange them according to my paper plan, but with plenty of latitude for changing pieces or altering my original idea. All fabrics, especially scrap mixtures, take on new dimensions when placed next to other fabrics, so you always need to make allowances just in case. Then you can move around and substitute pieces however you choose in order to achieve the design you have in mind or another design that suddenly presents itself.

Complete directions for an Attic Windows wall hanging are included in this book. Refer to Part 2 for essentials in fabric requirements, patterns, and step-by-step instructions.

Bow Tie

Like Attic Windows, the Bow Tie incorporates only two shapes—a square and a pentagon—to a unit, so it's a good choice for fabric mixtures. Each unit has five pieces (see Diagram 9). It is traditionally made with paired light and dark fabrics (in solids or prints) with a third fabric in the center square.

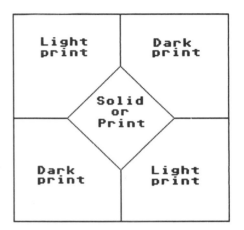

Diagram 9. Bow Tie (Basic Unit)

A Bow Tie can also be set in several ways; six different Bow Tie sets are described below. The set names are based on the visual impact of the Bow Tie unit—that is, how the viewer sets or sees the most prominent (usually the darkest) bow tie.

Traditional. The traditional setting (Diagram 10) of a pieced-scrap Bow Tie alternating with a plain square is fairly common. Without the right fabric mixtures, it can actually become humdrum. Even with striking fabric combinations in the pieced bow ties, the potential for creating a captivating secondary design is lost.

Horizontal. You can maximize the interaction of fabrics by setting them more directly against each other. Diagram 11 shows a horizontal Bow Tie, which is exactly that kind of setting. Even in this simple variation, the placement of units directly against each other adds new dimension.

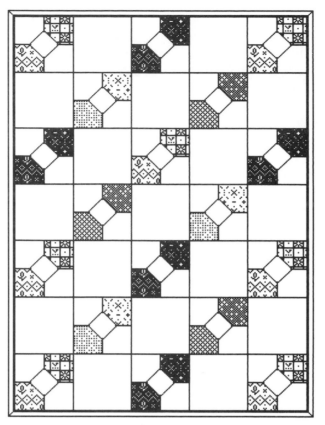

Diagram 10. Traditional Bow Tie Setting

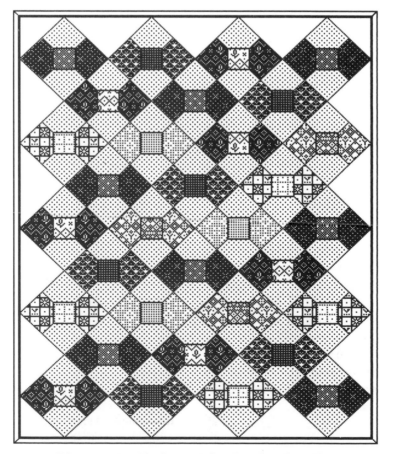

Diagram 11. Horizontal Setting for Bow Tie

33

Diagram 12. Vertical Setting for Bow Tie

Diagram 13. Diagonal Setting for Bow Tie

34

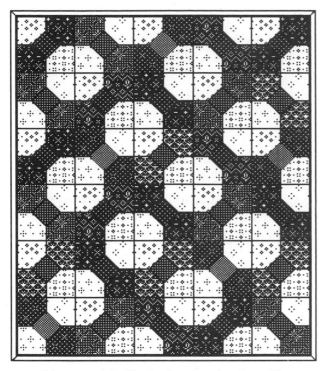

Diagram 14. Circle Setting for Bow Tie

Diagram 15. Random Setting for Bow Tie

The lighter part of the Bow Tie unit is placed end over end, emphasizing its diamond shape. The darkest ties appear in horizontal rows and seem more representational. You can even imagine the person or face or shirt in the background, adorned by the bow tie.

Vertical. By turning the units so that the darkest bow ties are connected in vertical columns, you produce a vertical set (Diagram 12). The eye is carried up and down because of the influence of the darker scraps.

Diagonal. The diagonal set (Diagram 13) is similar to the traditional set, except that the units are placed squarely against each other. Alternate plain squares have been eliminated. As in the traditional set, the bow ties are placed diagonally across the quilt surface, but their effect is more pronounced.

Circle. The circle set (Diagram 14) lends itself to innovative use of fabrics, more so than previously described sets. In addition to the primary Bow Tie design, a circle set features a secondary

latticework of light and dark octagons. Four Bow Tie units are placed with the darkest bows coming together to form an octagon. In the adjacent units, the light bows also come together in octagons. (These octagons resemble large circles more than angular shapes—hence the name of the set.) Several light and dark octagons across the quilt surface suggest latticework, the idea of peering through a dark grid into lighter space. The Bow Tie quilt pattern featured in this book is in the circle set.

Random. The sixth set variation (Diagram 15) is random, or mixed. In this setting, you may either give very little or considerable thought to placement of the bow ties. Because there is no patterned effect that the viewer can readily identify, perhaps achieving a successful scrap design in this set demands the greatest skill of all.

Outstanding color photographs of various Bow Tie sets can be found in several of the books listed in the Bibliography. See Chapter 6, "Some Traditional Patterns Suitable for Scrap Quilts," for specific Bow Tie references.

Your Turn

Though the layouts and sets have been described in relation to the Attic Windows and Bow Tie quilts, you can apply similar layouts and sets to *any* quilt pattern.

All of the diagrammed examples use windows and ties of the same proportion. There are no "correct" proportions, as you can see from Diagrams 16 and 17, which illustrate several size variations for Attic Windows and Bow Tie. An Attic Windows quilt with larger squares creates the illusion of shallowness. The same quilt with small squares gives the appearance of depth. A Bow Tie quilt with fairly large squares is imposing, while one with relatively small squares recedes. Find and use a variation that intrigues you.

Remember to select a simple pattern, but be adventurous: Consider a new or unusual setting and imagine that pattern and setting in your mixture of fabrics. Then start cutting and designing. Any initial apprehension will vanish as your imagination takes over and you explore the wealth of fascinating options that scrap quilting has to offer.

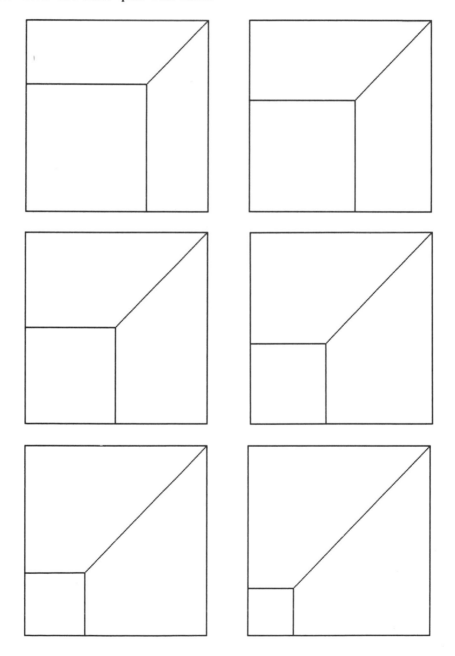

Diagram 16. Attic Windows in Several Proportions

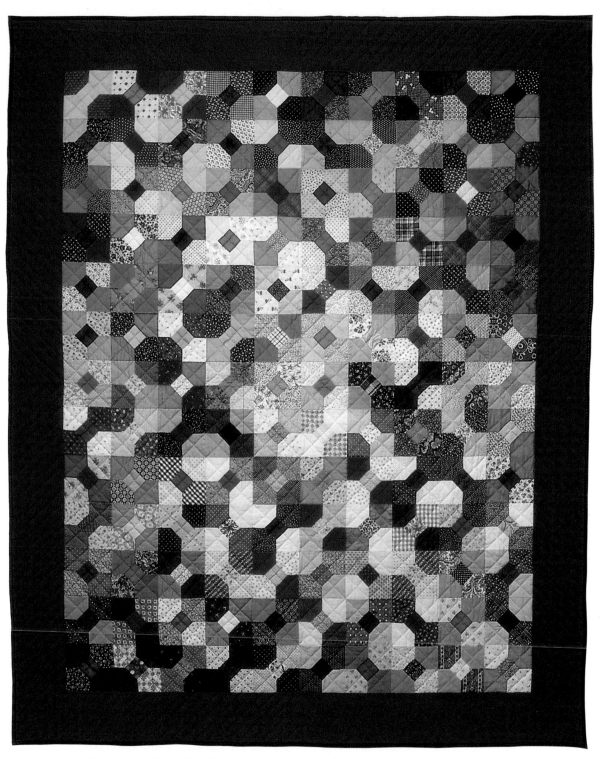

Bow Tie. 74″ × 92″. The effective use of color in Bow Tie adds interest in the form of a secondary design.

Quilt by the author and the Tuesday Quilters of Eau Claire, Wisconsin

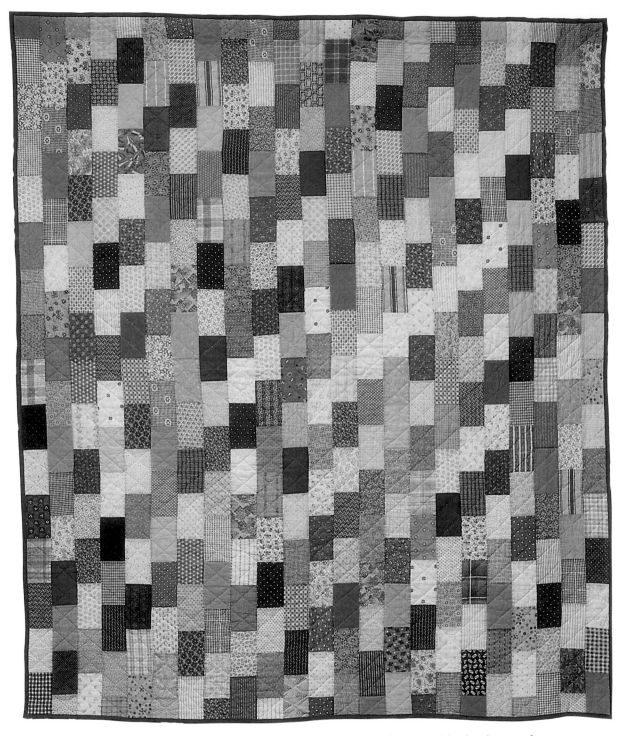

Brickwork. 69″ × 82″. Simplicity is the key to Brickwork: It's simple to make, and is built around a simple shape that works with all kinds of fabrics.
Quilt from the collection of Dr. and Mrs. J. Randall Dennison
Quilting by the author

Alphabetical by Flavor. 63″ × 84″. A whimsical, fun quilt—the idea behind
it will inspire all kinds of original adaptations.
Quilt by the author

Escape. 72″ × 90″. This 'Round the Twist variation communicates its theme in the interplay of light and dark solids and prints.
Quilt by Mary Mousel

Stars and Bars. 56″ × 72″. An example of how a basic fabric group—plaids—can generate an eye-catching, complex design.
Quilt by the author

Hole in the Barn Door. 56″ × 80″. Here's a quilt that's intricately pieced and carefully planned to feature a harmonious progression of color.
Quilt by Alice Weickelt

QUILTING DETAILS

Brickwork.

Alphabetical by Flavor.

Attic Windows.

Escape.

Bowtie.

Hole in the Barn Door.

Stars and Bars.

Attic Windows. 28½″ × 34½″. This setting is highlighted by "rays" of light-colored fabrics running diagonally across the quilt.
Quilt by the author

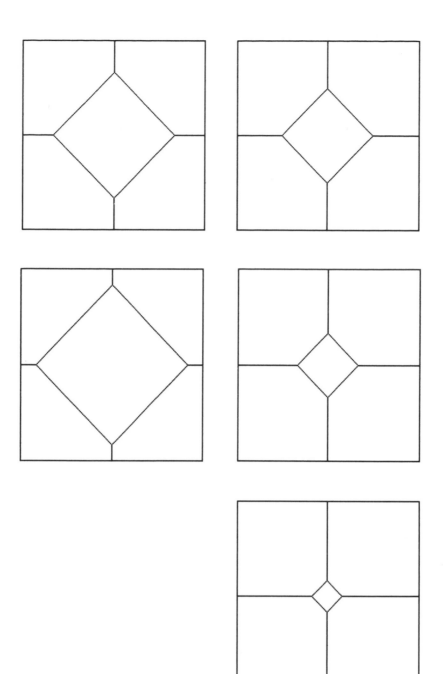

Diagram 17. Bow Tie in Several Proportions

6
Some Traditional Patterns Suitable for Scrap Quilts

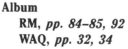

The patterns outlined in this chapter lend themselves well to effective overall designs, secondary designs, or in combination with other patterns. Several references are cited for each pattern. These references are for color pictures of fabric-mixture quilts using that pattern.

The patterns are sketched in black-and-white shapes only. This gives you more latitude both in selecting your fabrics and for planning your use of light, medium, and dark scraps. Select a pattern and copy it onto graph paper. Sketch in lights and darks. Draw several more. Adapt them and place them directly against each other, watching for secondary designs. Examples of this procedure are given in the preceding chapter, "Suggestions for Adapting Traditional Patterns."

Look at other illustrations and photographs throughout the book. Then check the reference table for other books in your personal, guild, or public library. The more successful fabric-mixture designs you study, the more ideas you can draw from in creating your own effective scrap quilts.

Note: Initials are given for 15 quilt book titles. See the Bibliography for publishing information.

Table 1. Reference Key

ACQ	*Amish Crib Quilts*
APQ	*American Patchwork & Quilting*
AWQ	*Award-Winning Quilts and How To Make Them*
CAB	*Calico and Beyond*
CBQ	*The Complete Book of Quiltmaking*
MQ	*Mennonite Quilts*
ND	*New Discoveries in American Quilts*
RM	*Remember Me*
PQ	*The Pieced Quilt*
QEC	*Quilt Engagement Calendars*
QPA	*Quilting, Patchwork & Appliqué*
SAQ	*The State of the Art Quilt*
SQ	*Scrap Quilts*
SL	*The Scrap Look*
WAQ	*The World of Amish Quilts*

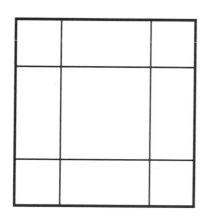

Album
RM, *pp. 84–85, 92*
WAQ, *pp. 32, 34*

Four-Patch Album
APQ, *p. 201*
CBQ, *p. 139*
RM, *pp. 50–51, 119*
SL, *p. 107*

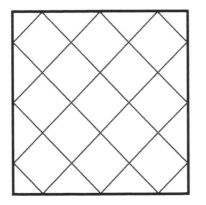

Nine-Patch Album
  ND, *p. 51*
  RM, *pp. 12–13, 17, 100*
  SL, *pp. 108–9*

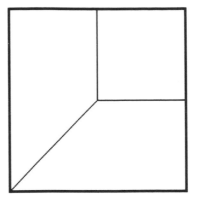

Attic Windows
  CAB, *pl. 13-B*
  PQ, *pl. 73*

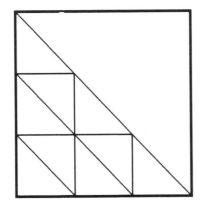

Birds in Air
  APQ, *p. 124*
  CAB, *p. 29*
  PQ, *pl. 76*
  QEC (1980), *#30*

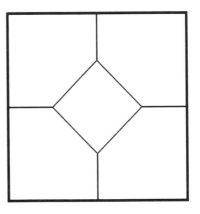

Bow Tie
  ACQ, *pp. 2, 40*
  APQ, *p. 190*
  QEC (1979), *#11, #39*
      (1982), #48
  WAQ, *pp. 88–90*

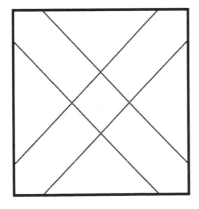

Crossroads
  RM, *pp. 62–63, 70–71*
  QEC (1987), *#10*

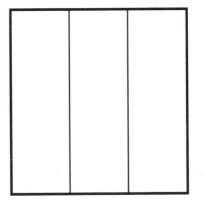

Fence Posts
  ACQ, *p. 33*
  APQ, *p. 34*
  PQ, *pl. 70*
  WAQ, *pp. 109, 113*

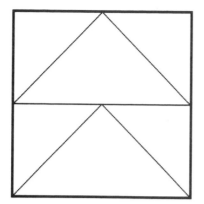

Flying Geese
ND, *p. 18*
QEC (1977), *#48*
(1983), *#24*
(1986), *#20*
(1987), *#42*
WAQ, *p. 30*

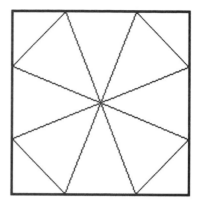

Kaleidoscope
CAB, *pl. 5-A*
PQ, *pl. 16*

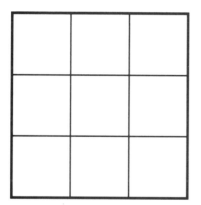

Nine-Patch Squares
APQ, *p. 183*
QEC (1978), *#20*
(1982), *#20*
(1983), *#15*
(1985), *#18, #30, #53*
(1986), *#44*
QPA, *pp. 71, 73*
WAQ, *p. 35*

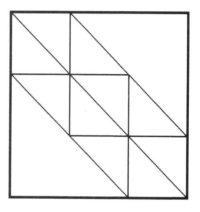

North Winds
APQ, *pp. 68, 124*
QEC (1984), *#32*

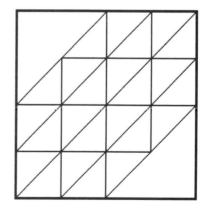

Ocean Waves
APQ, *p. 43*
MQ, *p. 69*
ND, *pp. 58–59*
QEC (1983), *#12, #45, #48*
(1984), *#3, #57*
QPA, *p. 86*
SL, *p. 37*
WAQ, *pp. 2, 76–79*

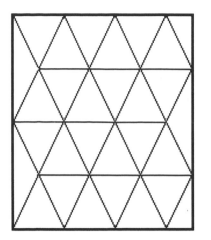

Pyramids
    APQ, *p. 130*
    PQ, *pl. 29*
    QEC (1980), *#51*
        (1983), *#33*
        (1984), *#13*
    SL, *p. 40*

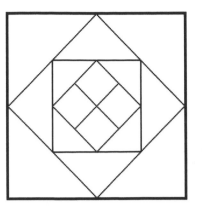

Snail's Tail
    ACQ, *p. 43*
    MQ, *p. 9*
    QEC (1984), *#6*
    SQ, *p. 59*
    WAQ, *p. 125*

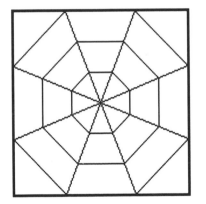

Spider Web
    ND, *p. 38*
    PQ, *pl. 81, 82, 94*
    QEC (1978), *#22*

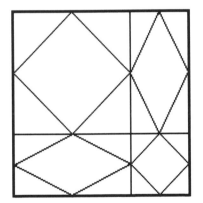

Storm at Sea
    SAQ, *p. 48*
    SQ, *p. 35*

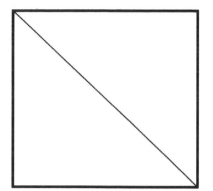

Triangles

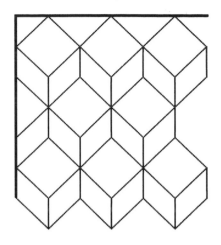

Elongated Tumbling Blocks

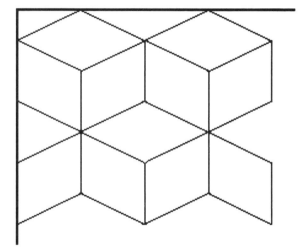

Tumbling Blocks

Part 2
The Quilts

7
Attic Windows

For Starters

The following list will help you enjoy a smooth start and steady progress in your work on Attic Windows. It contains a variety of general information about making the quilt.

- **Wash** and **press** all fabrics, including scraps, before you begin.
- For **templates** (patterns of the quilt pieces), use sturdy plastic or sandpaper, and be sure to note grain-line arrows.
- For the **squares** and the **border**, the quilt shown uses a medium shade and a dark shade (respectively) of the same color.
- **Seam width** is ¼".
- **Piecing** may be done by machine or hand.

    For **machine** piecing, include the ¼" seam allowances *with* the templates.

    For **hand** piecing, make the templates *without* seam allowances and add them when marking and cutting the fabrics.
- The **finished size** for Attic Windows is 28½" × 34½" (or 34½" × 28½", if you choose to hang it horizontally).
- The **border** measures 1¾" wide.
- The **blocks** (a total of 20) measure 6" square each.

Supplies

Quilt top fabric
Use 44"/45"-wide cotton or cotton/polyester blends.

Medium shade (for squares): ⅜ yard.

Dark shade (for borders): 1 yard.

Scraps: Use a variety of dark and light scraps. Try to get as many as 20 different light scraps, and do the same for dark scraps. Minimum scrap size is 7" square. If you're buying new fabric, the minimum cut needed is ⅛ yard of each fabric. And remember—the more variety, the better.

Backing and binding
You'll need 1¾ yards good-quality unbleached muslin or light solid-color fabric compatible with the other fabrics you're using in the quilt.

Batting
Choose either crib batting (45" × 60") or a piece of bonded polyester (30" × 36").

Other supplies

iron	natural-color quilting thread
quilting needles	(1 spool)
pins	sewing thread
ruler	thread for basting
scissors	soap chips or marking pencils
thimble	template material

Optional: Hoop or frame for quilting.

Ready to Work

Cutting
Before you begin cutting out quilt pieces, make templates from patterns AW-1 (square) and AW-2 (trapezoid), which are found at the end of this chapter. (*AW* stands for *Attic Windows.*)

Then, from the darker fabric you've chosen, cut the borders (border measurements *include* allowances for seams and mitering): You need two end borders, 2¼" × 28", and two side borders, 2¼" × 34".

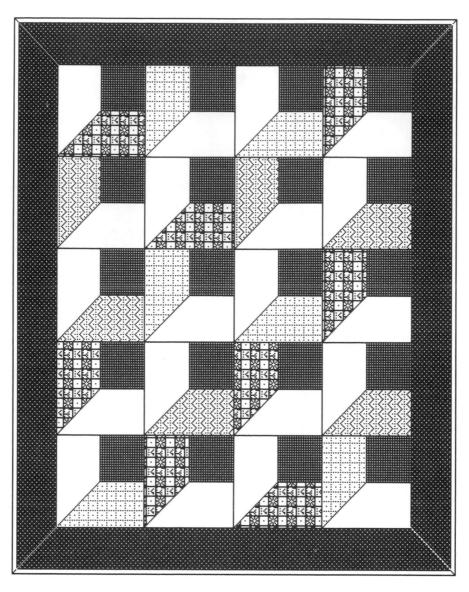

Diagram 1. Attic Windows Layout

Next, cut 20 squares (AW-1) from the medium-shade fabric.

From the variety of dark scraps, cut 10 trapezoids (AW-2). Reverse the template (turn it upside down) and cut 10 more, for a total of 20 dark scrap trapezoids.

From the light scraps, cut 20 trapezoids the same way you cut them from the dark scraps (10 regular, 10 reverse).

Design suggestions

On a large flat surface, lay all cut pieces (right side up) in a layout similar to the one used in Diagram 1. Experiment with arrangements that blend the scraps and solids to give the three-dimensional "window" effect and the diagonal "log cabin" effect. When a design is selected, group pieces into 20 six-inch units, each consisting of a square and a dark and light scrap, as in Diagram 2. Ten of these will have the dark and light scraps in opposite positions.

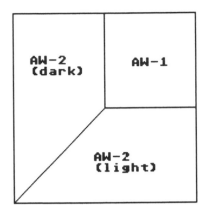

Diagram 2. Basic Attic Windows Unit

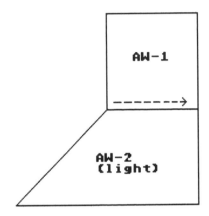

Diagram 3. Attic Windows Piecing—Step 1

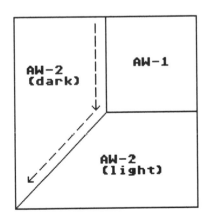

Diagram 4. Pivot Seam to Complete Attic Windows Unit

Scraps No More

Assembly

To assemble, first piece a square (AW-1) to the bottom trapezoid (AW-2), as in Diagram 3. Then join the second trapezoid in a pivot seam as indicated by the arrows in Diagram 4. Press seams to one side. Piece 19 more units in a similar fashion.

Join four units to make a row. Make five rows and join them in long crosswise seams.

Add the borders, mitering the corners, as in Diagram 1.

Quilting

From backing material, cut a 30″ × 36″ piece. Place this right side down. Lay the batting and pieced top (right side up) over it. Pin or thread-baste the three layers together, about every 3 or 4 inches.

With a straightedge and soap chip, mark diagonal crosshatch quilting lines, as in Diagram 5. Quilt with natural-color quilting thread.

Finishing

Trim the batting to ½″ larger than the quilt top, to allow for filler in the binding. Trim the quilt backing to match the top. From the remaining backing fabric, mark and cut 3″-wide bias strips (for a finished binding about ½″ wide). Fold the binding, wrong sides together, and attach it to the quilt front, making sure that the seam goes through all the layers. Turn the binding to the back of the quilt and whipstitch it in place.

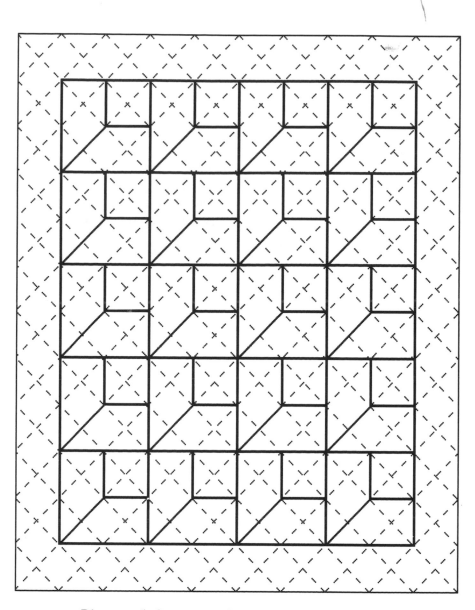

Diagram 5. Suggested Quilting for Attic Windows

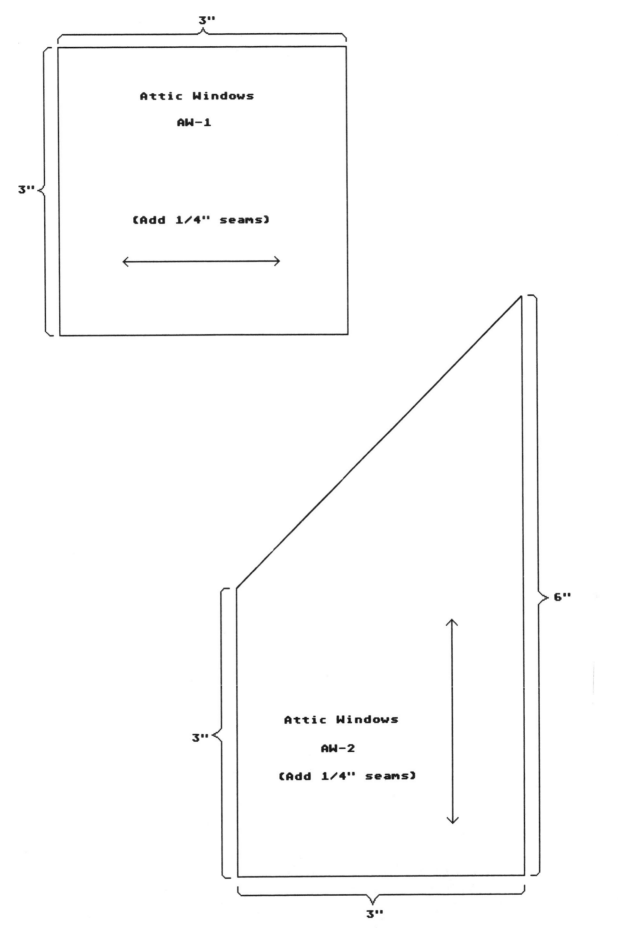

3"

Attic Windows

AW-1

(Add 1/4" seams)

3"

←——————→

6"

Attic Windows

AW-2

(Add 1/4" seams)

3"

3"

59

8
Bow Tie

For Starters

The following list will help you enjoy a smooth start and steady progress in your work on Bow Tie. It contains a variety of general information about making the quilt.

- **Wash** and **press** all fabrics, including scraps, before you begin.
- For **templates** (patterns of the quilt pieces), use sturdy plastic or sandpaper, and be sure to note grain-line arrows.
- The **border** of the Bow Tie shown is a deep burgundy; the **binding** shown is made from a black print. As usual, you should choose the colors which best enhance the colors of the quilt top you're planning.
- **Seam width** is ¼".
- **Piecing** may be done by machine or hand.

    For **machine** piecing, include the ¼" seam allowances *with* the templates.

    For **hand** piecing, make the templates *without* seam allowances and add them when marking and cutting the fabrics.
- The **finished size** for Bow Tie is 74" × 92".

Supplies

Quilt top fabric
Use 44"/45"-wide cotton or cotton/polyester blends.

Borders: 2¾ yards (your choice of color).

Scraps: Choose from a wide variety of prints and solids for a total of about 3 yards each of dark and light scraps. The minimum scrap size is about 3" × 3" for the center of each bow tie and 4" × 8" for a pair of the larger pieces of the bow tie.

Backing
You'll need 5¾ yards of good-quality unbleached muslin.

Binding
Bow Tie calls for 1 yard of binding fabric (again, your choice of color).

Batting
Use 81" × 96" of bonded polyester.

Other supplies

iron	quilting thread (2 spools;
quilting needles	match with border color)
pins	sewing thread (a medium
long straightedge	neutral color)
scissors	thread for basting
thimble	soap chips or marking pencils
	template material

Optional: Hoop or frame for quilting.

Ready to Work

Cutting
Begin by cutting out the templates from patterns A and B, found at the end of this chapter. From scrap fabrics, cut 130 A pieces (squares). Then cut 520 B pieces (trapezoids) in matched pairs (260 pairs).

It may be easier to assemble fabrics in groups of three compatible colors/prints, including both lights and darks. If you take this approach, you'll cut the center square from one fabric, and the four trapezoids required to complete the block from the other two fabrics (two of each). In any case, the total number of pieces to cut is 650.

From the border fabric you've selected, cut two side—7″ × 91½″—and two end—7″ × 73½″—borders. Remember that for borders, allowances for seams and mitering are *included* in the measurements given.

Piecing the Bow Tie units

Gather the five pieces that constitute a Bow Tie unit. With right sides together, join piece B to one side of the center square (piece A—see Diagram 1). Likewise, add the opposite B piece (see Diagram 2). Finally, join each of the remaining B pieces to the center square. To do this, use a pivot seam: Beginning at the outside of piece B, stitch toward the center square; then stitch across the adjacent side of the square, and back to the outside of piece B (as indicated by the arrows in Diagram 3).

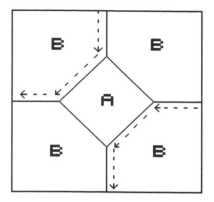

Diagram 3. Pivot Seam to Complete Bow Tie Unit

Continue piecing until you've made 130 Bow Tie units. Each unit will measure 6″ square without seam allowances.

Design suggestions

Lay out all units on a large flat surface (table, bed, floor, or working wall). Arrange blocks in a format that permits maximum contrast among light and dark fabrics. Try several arrangements.

To get the effect of light and dark gridwork, place four of the bow tie designs with the darkest fabrics coming together to form a dark octagon, as in Diagram 4. Fill in the block with additional ties so that the light trapezoids touch the light parts of neighboring bow ties. Then, when another block is added, the light trapezoids will form an octagon of light fabrics, as in Diagram 5. Continue placing bow tie units with fabrics grouped together to form light and dark octagons, and you'll see a graphic diagonal gridwork. The Bow Tie quilt pictured in this book features such a design.

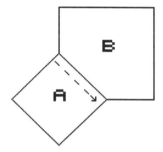

Diagram 1. Bow Tie Piecing—Step 1

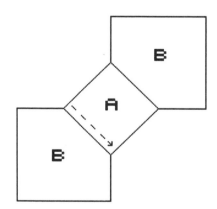

Diagram 2. Bow Tie Piecing—Step 2

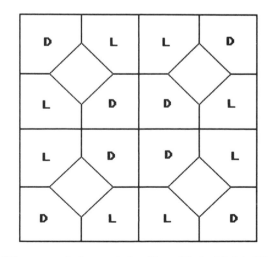

Diagram 4. Layout for Bow Tie's Light (L) and Dark (D) Units

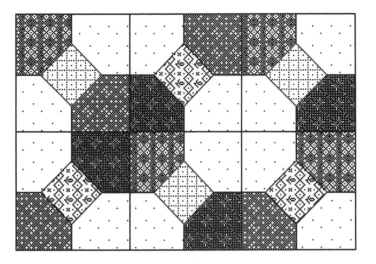

Diagram 5. The Light Octagon in Bow Tie

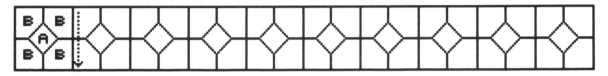

Diagram 6. Bow Tie, Row 1

Try several other Bow Tie layouts as described in the "Bow Tie" section of Chapter 5, "Suggestions for Adapting Traditional Patterns." For the Bow Tie quilt, these may include vertical, horizontal, diagonal, alternate block, circle, and random sets.

Be sure to try all the interesting possibilities for your complete quilt top design before you begin joining the Bow Tie blocks together.

Scraps No More

Assembly
Gather units by row, beginning with row 1, as in Diagram 6. Each row contains ten blocks. Piece the ten blocks to form row 1.

Continue piecing to form rows 2 through 13. Join the rows using long, crosswise seams. Finally, add side borders and end borders, mitering the corners. The completed top is shown in Diagram 7.

Quilting
From the 5¾ yards of backing fabric, cut two 99" lengths. Keep one piece intact (about 42" wide). From the other piece, cut two 18" widths. Using ¼" seams, join a split width to each side of the intact center panel. Press seams toward the outside. Place quilt backing right side down. Smooth the batting over it. Place the pressed quilt top over the batting, right side up. Pin or baste the three layers together for quilting.

Mark diagonal quilting lines with a straight-edge and soap chip or marking pencil, according to Diagram 8. Quilt along all marked lines.

Finishing
Trim the batting to ½" larger than the quilt top, to allow for filler in the binding. Trim the quilt backing to match the size of the top. To make the bias binding (from the yard of fabric you've chosen—the quilt shown uses a black print), first mark and cut 3"-wide bias strips. Fold the binding, wrong sides together, and attach it to the quilt front in a ¼" seam that goes through all the layers. Finally, turn the binding to the back of the quilt and whipstitch it in place. The finished binding should be about ½" wide.

63

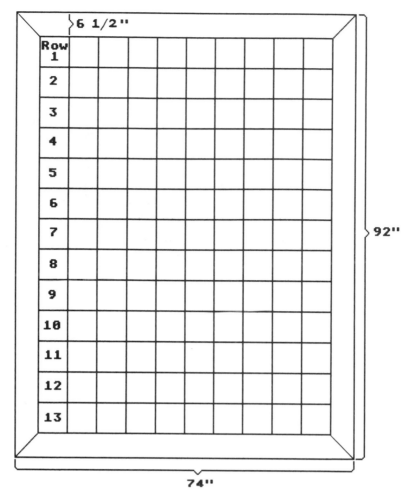

Diagram 7. Completely Pieced Top for Bow Tie

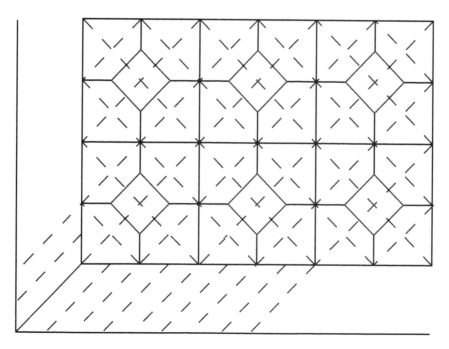

Diagram 8. Suggested Quilting for Bow Tie

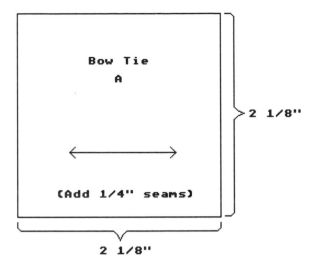

Bow Tie
A

←——————→

(Add 1/4" seams)

2 1/8"

2 1/8"

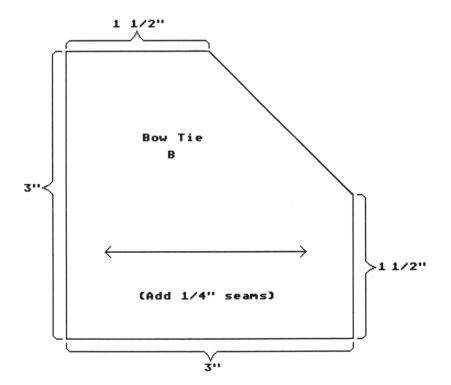

1 1/2"

Bow Tie
B

3"

1 1/2"

←——————————————→

(Add 1/4" seams)

3"

9
Brickwork

For Starters

The following list will help you enjoy a smooth start and steady progress in your work on this quilt. It contains a variety of general information about making Brickwork.

- **Wash** and **press** all fabrics, including scraps, before you begin.
- For **templates** (patterns of the quilt pieces), use sturdy plastic or sandpaper, and be sure to note grain-line arrows.
- The **binding** for the quilt shown is dark blue, but you should choose the shade that best highlights the colors present in the scraps you're using.
- **Seam width** is ¼″.
- **Piecing** may be done by machine or hand.

   For **machine** piecing, include the ¼″ seam allowances *with* the templates.

   For **hand** piecing, make the templates *without* seam allowances and add them when marking and cutting the fabrics.
- The **finished size** for Brickwork is 69″ × 82″.

Supplies

Quilt top fabric
Use 44″/45″-wide cotton or cotton/polyester blends.

Scraps: Include prints and solids to total about 4 yards each of dark and light scraps. Use as much variety as you can. The minimum scrap size is a rectangle about 4″ × 6″.

Backing
This requires 5¼ yards of good-quality unbleached muslin.

Binding
Use 1 yard of any solid-color fabric that complements your scrap mixture.

Batting
You'll need 72″ × 90″ (twin size) bonded polyester.

Other supplies

iron	natural-color quilting thread
long straightedge	(2 spools)
pins	sewing thread (a medium
quilting needles	neutral color)
scissors	thread for basting
thimble	soap chips or marking pencils
	template material

Optional: Hoop or frame for quilting.

Ready to Work

Cutting
First cut out the templates; these are the two rectangular patterns found at the end of this chapter.

Then divide all your fabrics into two groups: light and dark. (Hold fabrics next to each other to compare the amount of light and dark in each.) Work toward getting about the same number of fabrics in each pile.

From the dark scraps, cut 175 large rectangles and 10 small rectangles. Do likewise in cutting from the light scraps. This will give you the required 345 large rectangles and 15 small rectangles, plus a few extras.

Design suggestions
Again, group fabric pieces into two piles: one light and one dark. On a large working surface, begin laying out pieces in vertical rows, alternating the lights and darks (see Diagram 1). Lay out a portion of the quilt to get an impression of the mixture of

fabrics and of the interplay among rows. Note the diagonal formation of the "brickwork." Study the layout from a distance (stand back and squint), or look through the viewfinder of a camera or the reverse end of a pair of binoculars to see the design in miniature. Move fabric pieces freely about to determine the concentrations of light and dark that you prefer.

The Brickwork quilt featured in this book is basically a diagonal layout (see Diagram 2) of alternate light and dark fabrics. Otherwise—in terms of the print and color of each fabric—the pieces are randomly selected and placed. You could give more emphasis to color arrangement by grouping certain color tones in diagonal paths or by concentrating colors in specific areas.

Scraps No More

Assembly
Brickwork is arranged and assembled in 23 vertical rows. Begin row 1 with a small, light rectangle (see Diagram 1). The remaining 15 rectangles are large ones pieced lengthwise into the row—with dark and light pieces alternated.

Piece rows 2 through 23 likewise, alternating dark and light fabrics. Begin row 2 with a large, dark rectangle; it will end with a small, light one. Begin row 3 with a small, dark rectangle, row 4 with a large, light one, and so on, according to Diagram 2.

After you've pieced the 23 vertical rows, join them in long vertical seams to complete the 69″ × 82″ top.

Quilting
From the 5¼ yards of backing fabric, cut two 90″ lengths. Keep one intact (about 42″ wide). From the other piece, cut two 16″ widths. Using ¼″ seams, join a split width to each side of the intact center panel. Press seams toward the outside.

Place the quilt backing right side down. Smooth the batting over it. Place the pressed quilt top over the batting, right side up. Pin or baste the three layers together for quilting.

Mark diagonal lines with a long straightedge and soap chip or marking pencil, according to Diagram 3.

(Top)

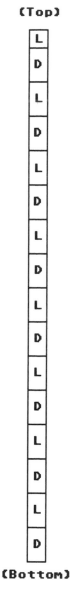

(Bottom)

Diagram 1. Pattern of Light (L) and Dark (D) Pieces in Brickwork, Row 1

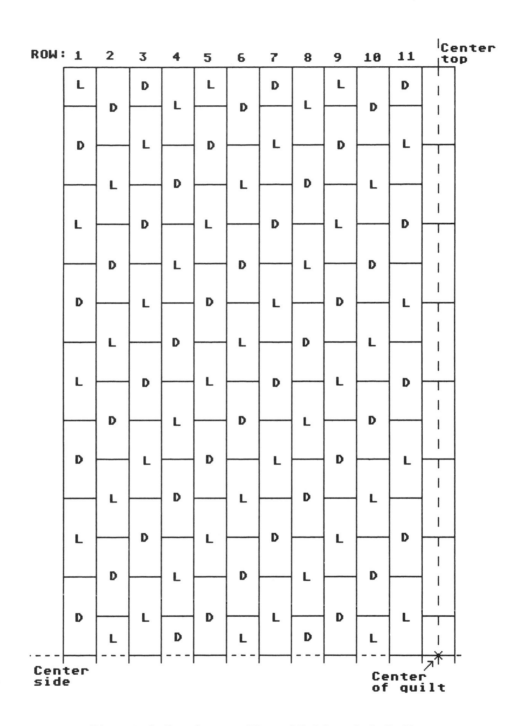

Diagram 2. One-Quarter View of Brickwork Quilt Top

69

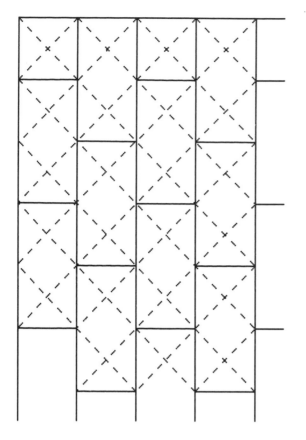

Diagram 3. Suggested Quilting for Brickwork

Finishing

Trim the batting so that it's ½″ larger than the quilt top, to allow for filler in the binding. Trim the quilt backing to match the top. Mark and cut 3″-wide bias strips (for a finished binding about ½″ wide) from the yard of fabric you've chosen. Fold the binding, wrong sides together, and attach it to the quilt front, making sure that the seam goes through all the layers. Turn the binding to the back of the quilt and whipstitch it in place.

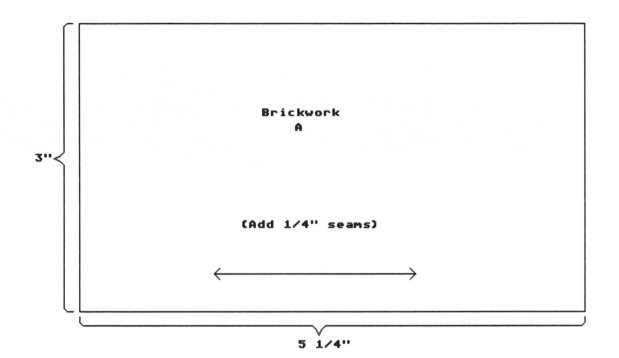

Brickwork
A

(Add 1/4" seams)

3"

5 1/4"

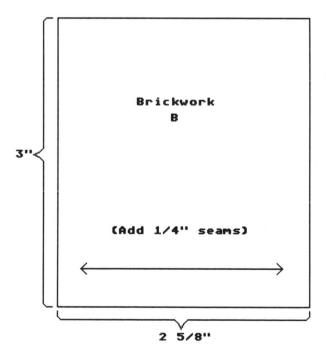

Brickwork
B

(Add 1/4" seams)

3"

2 5/8"

10
Alphabetical by Flavor

For Starters

The following list will help you enjoy a smooth start and steady progress in your work on Alphabetical by Flavor. It contains a variety of general information about making the quilt.

- **Wash** and **press** all fabrics, including scraps, before you begin.
- For the **template** (pattern of the quilt pieces), use sturdy plastic or sandpaper, and be sure to note grain-line arrows.
- Alphabetical by Flavor employs a **background** along with the pieced sections of the top.
- For the **border**, the quilt shown uses a cinnamon shade; the **binding** is a medium shade of blue. The instructions below assume that you will also use those colors, but you may prefer different ones, depending on the "flavors" you're actually able to incorporate into your quilt.
- **Seam width** is ¼″.
- **Piecing** may be done by machine or hand.

    For **machine** piecing, include the ¼″ seam allowances *with* the templates.

    For **hand** piecing, make the templates *without* seam allowances and add them when marking and cutting the fabrics.
- The **finished size** for Alphabetical by Flavor is 63″ × 84″.

Supplies

Quilt top fabric
Use 100-percent cotton (44″/45″ wide).

Scraps: The pieced rectangles require 132 cotton solids, each a different color. Minimum scrap size is 4″ × 7″. If you're buying new fabrics, the minimum cut is ⅛ yard of each one.

Background: 2 yards of good-quality unbleached muslin.

Borders: 2½ yards (cinnamon-color; see "For Starters" for note about border and binding colors).

Binding
You'll need 1 yard of blue (a medium shade) fabric for the binding.

Backing
This calls for 5 yards of good-quality unbleached muslin.

Batting
Use 72″ × 90″ (twin size) bonded polyester.

Other supplies

iron	quilting thread (2 spools—
long straightedge	your choice of color)
pins	sewing thread (a medium
quilting needles	neutral color)
scissors	thread for basting
thimble	soap chips or marking pencils
	template material

Optional: Hoop or frame for quilting.

Ready to Work

Cutting
After you've made the rectangle template (found at the end of this chapter), cut 132 pieces, each from a different color.

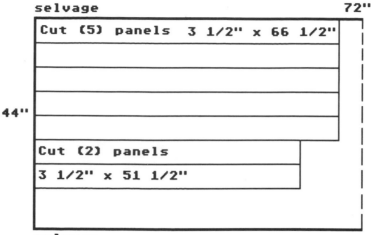

Diagram 1. Alphabetical by Flavor:
Layout for Background Fabric
(not shown to scale)

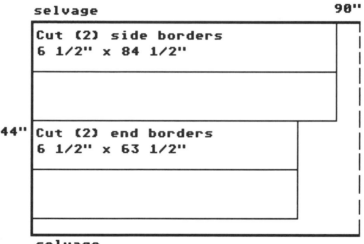

Diagram 2. Alphabetical by Flavor:
Layout for Border Fabric
(not shown to scale)

Cut the following background strips, as indicated in Diagram 1 (these measurements *include* seam allowances):

5 panels, 3½″ × 66½″ each
2 panels (for top and bottom of quilt top),
    3½″ × 51½″ each

From the cinnamon-color fabric, cut the following borders, as indicated in Diagram 2 (again, these measurements *include* seam allowances):

2 side borders, 6½″ × 84½″ each

2 end borders, 6½″ × 63½″ each

Design suggestions

Alphabetical by Flavor is, as its name suggests, a quilt designed to convey a flavor theme through its color design; each color represents a specific flavor or taste. Because this quilt incorporates so many different colors—each of which must be a solid, and 100-percent cotton—you'll probably have to ask friends to help contribute scraps for it.

For my quilt, I made a long list of flavors such as candies, spices, seasonings, fruits, and ice cream. Then I began to pair each flavor with an appropriate color. This process eliminated several flavors that didn't have a compatible color. (I also scratched a few from the list just because I didn't particularly care for them, or because they seemed a little bland—flavors like custard, muskmelon, French vanilla, allspice, and penuche.)

After experimenting with the pressure and effects (including its durability when washed) of typing on the fabric, I used a typewriter to label the "flavor" of each fabric piece. At this point several more fabric colors had to be discarded because they were too dark to show the typed information clearly: dark browns, purples, and black, for instance, which affected flavors such as coffee, rum, and licorice.

My Flavors quilt is arranged alphabetically, which is certainly a straightforward way to set the rectangles. There are six columns, each with 22 colors (see Table 1).

You could also group fabrics by colors, beginning at one end of the color spectrum and working toward the other end (reds, oranges, yellows, greens, blues, indigoes, and violets). Or you could work with an arrangement based on light and dark fabrics, perhaps alternating light and dark rectangles or columns, or working for gradual progressions of color intensity across the entire quilt. The Flavors theme can be eliminated entirely as you work only with the colors to develop a layout that you consider attractive and pleasing.

Scraps No More

Assembly
Each of the six columns in Alphabetical by Flavor measures 6″ × 66″. Begin with the rectangle at the top of a column and add the piece immediately below it, remembering to use a ¼″ seam. Continue adding rectangles to complete a column of 22 fabrics, as in Diagram 3. Then make five more columns.

To complete the quilt top, place a 3½″-wide muslin panel between each of the pieced columns, as in Diagram 4 (without seam allowances, each

Table 1. Alphabetical by Flavor Arrangement

Ambrosia	Brandy	Creme de Menthe	Honey	Oregano	Rosemary
Anise	Bubble Gum	Cucumber	Honeydew	Parsley	Ruby Pear
Apricot	Burgundy	Currant	Ice Blue Mint	Peach	Sage
Artichoke	Butter Pecan	Damson	Jalapeño Pepper	Peanut Butter	Spearmint
Avocado	Butterscotch	Dandelion	Lemon-Lime	Pear	Strawberry
Banana	Candied Fruit	Date	Lemon Meringue	Peppermint	Sugar Plum
Bing Cherry	Candy Apple	Dewberry	Lime	Pineapple	Tangerine
Blackberry Ice	Cantaloupe	Dill	Loganberry	Pink Lemonade	Tarragon
Blackberry Ripple	Caramel	Double Cherry	Mandarin	Pistachio	Thyme
Blackberry Swirl	Celeriac	Elderberry	Mango	Plum	Toasted Almond
Black Raspberry	Celery	Eucalyptus	Maple Nut	Pomegranate	Toasted Coconut
Blueberry	Champagne	Fudge	Marjoram	Port Wine	Toffee
Blueberry Buckle	Chocolate	Ginger	Marmalade	Praline	Tokay
Blueberry Ice	Chokecherry	Golden Delicious	Melon	Prune	Tropical Plum
Blueberry Ripple	Cinnamon	Gooseberry	Mint	Pumpkin	Tutti-Frutti
Blueberry Swirl	Citron	Grape	Mocha	Punch	Watermelon
Blue Cheese	Cocoa	Grapefruit	Mossberry	Raspberry	Wild Cherry
Blue Plum	Concord	Green Apple	Mulberry	Red Delicious	Wild Strawberry
Bonbon	Cotton Candy	Green Grape	Mulled Cider	Rhubarb	Wine
Boysenberry	Crab Apple	Green Onion	Nectarine	Rhubarbagrote	Wintergreen
Boysenberry Ice	Cranberry	Green Pepper	Nutmeg	Root Beer	Vanilla
Boysenberry Ripple	Cranberry Ice	Gumdrop	Orange	Roquefort	Youngberry

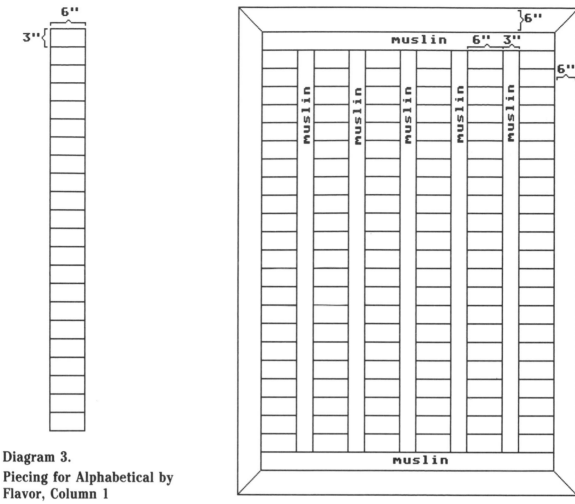

Diagram 3.
Piecing for Alphabetical by Flavor, Column 1

Diagram 4. Alphabetical by Flavor: Complete Layout of Quilt Top

panel will measure 3″ wide). Next, add the shorter 3½″ muslin panels, one at the top and one at the bottom of the quilt. Finally, add the 6″ borders to the sides and ends of the quilt, mitering all corners.

Quilting

From the five yards of backing fabric, cut two 90″ lengths. Keep one piece intact (about 42″ wide). From the other piece cut two 14″ widths. Join a split width to each side of the intact center panel. Press seams toward the outside.

Place quilt backing right side down. Smooth the batting over it. Place the pressed quilt top over the batting, right side up. Pin or baste the three layers together for quilting. Mark the quilt top with gentle flowing curves and swirls to "blend" the flavors together, as in Diagram 5. It is easiest

to mark these curved lines with a fine soap chip, making large circular motions as you mark. Strive for a similar amount of quilting throughout: It's easy to end up with areas that are over- or underquilted when you mark randomly, as with this design. Use quilting thread in a color of your choice, or try a mixture of colors to contribute to the blended effect.

Finishing

Trim the batting so that it's ½″ larger than the quilt top, to allow for filler in the binding. Then trim the quilt backing to match the top. From the yard of medium-blue fabric, mark and cut 3″-wide bias strips (for a finished binding about ½″ wide). Fold the binding, wrong sides together, and attach it to the quilt front so that the seam penetrates all the layers. Turn the binding to the back of the quilt and whipstitch it in place.

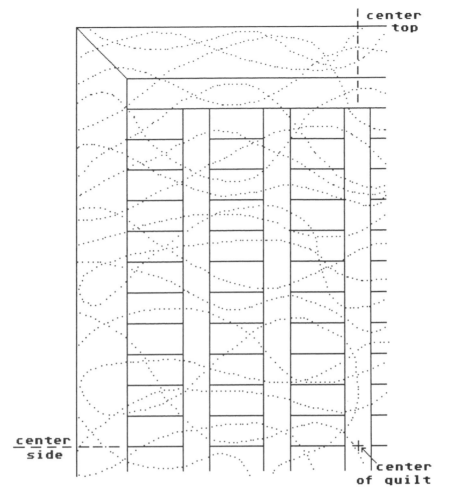

center top

center side

center
of quilt

Diagram 5. Suggested Quilting for
Alphabetical by Flavor (One-Quarter View)

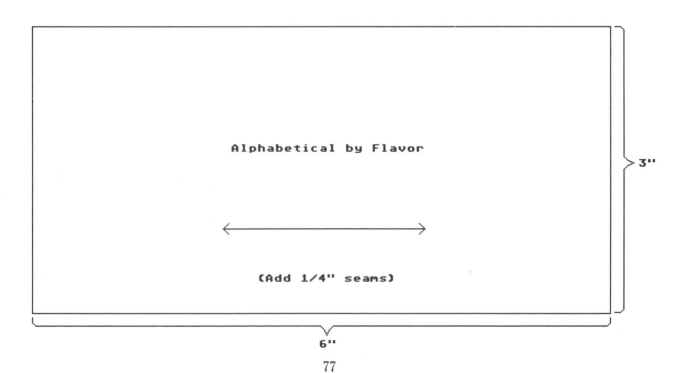

Alphabetical by Flavor

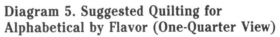

(Add 1/4" seams)

3"

6"

11
Hole in the Barn Door

Quilt by Alice Weickelt

For Starters

The following list will help you enjoy a smooth start and steady progress in your work on Hole in the Barn Door. It contains a variety of general information about making the quilt.

- **Wash** and **press** all fabrics, including scraps, before you begin.
- For **templates** (patterns of the quilt pieces), use sturdy plastic or sandpaper, and be sure to note grain-line arrows.
- This quilt is constructed in **rows**, rather than blocks. For construction purposes, think of the design as composed of 18 horizontal rows, designated A through R, as in Diagram 1.
- **X** (in the diagrams for Hole in the Barn Door) refers to the background fabric.
- **Seam width** is ¼".
- **Piecing** may be done by machine or hand.

     For **machine** piecing, include the ¼" seam allowances *with* the templates.

     For **hand** piecing, make the templates *without* seam allowances and add them when marking and cutting the fabrics.
- The **finished size** for Hole in the Barn Door is 56" × 80".

Supplies

Quilt top fabric

Use 44"/45"-wide cotton or cotton/polyester blends.

Scraps: Twenty-eight different fabric prints are needed to piece the top for Hole in the Barn Door. Select an array of prints that blend gradually from one color to the next. The quilt featured here works from top to bottom, using 28 prints in shades of salmon, pink, blue, tan, brown, rose, orchid, green, gold, and rust. A broad range of colors keeps the design from becoming monotonous. In addition, try to find a variety of fine, medium, and bold prints.

In general, you will need about ¼ yard each of the 28 prints. You will need only about ⅛ yard of certain fabrics, however, so some of your scrap pieces that are smaller than ¼ yard may be adequate; try those with the fabrics numbered 2, 7, 12, 17, 22, and 27.

Background and borders: 2¼ yards light-colored fine print or solid.

Binding

You need 1 yard of fabric; the quilt pictured uses a medium-tan print, but as usual, you should select the color that best complements the scraps used in your quilt top.

Backing

Hole in the Barn Door requires 5 yards of good-quality muslin for backing.

Batting

Use 72" × 90" (twin size) bonded polyester.

Other supplies

iron	2 spools natural-color quilting
long straightedge	thread
pins	sewing thread (a medium
quilting needles	neutral color)
scissors	thread for basting
thimble	soap chips or marking pencils
	template material

Optional: Hoop or frame for quilting.

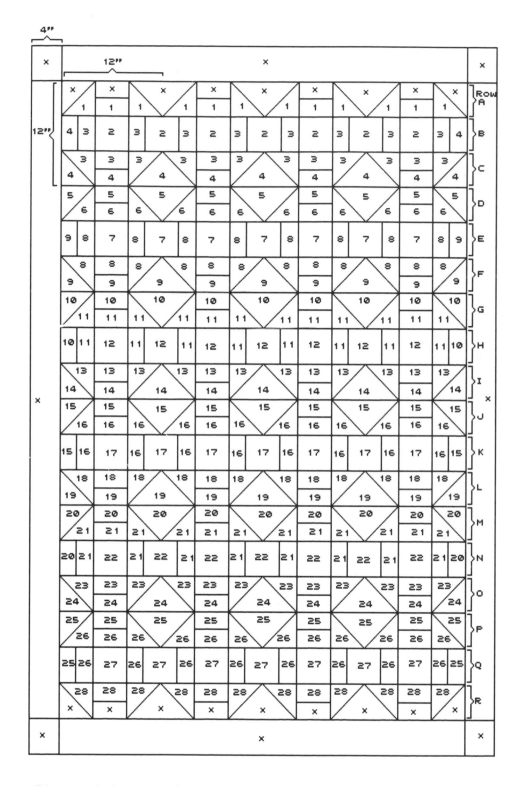

Diagram 1. Layout and Numbering of Fabrics in Hole in the Barn Door

80

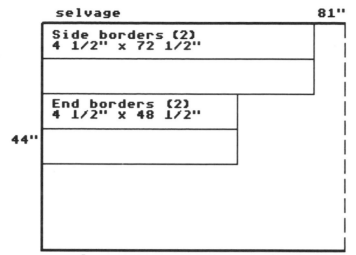

**Diagram 2. Layout for Background/Border
Fabric in Hole in the Barn Door**
(not shown to scale)

Ready to Work

Design suggestions

For this quilt, you must consider design before cutting any of the pieces: The pieces cannot be cut until each fabric is labeled, and the fabric cannot be labeled until you have decided how you will arrange it.

Lay the background fabric on a large, flat working surface. Gather the 28 print fabrics and arrange each one horizontally against the background fabric; generally, you want the vertical sequence to move gently from color to color. (See the photograph for the Hole in the Barn Door quilt featured in this book.) Move the fabrics around to see other possible color sequences. Make substitutions for any fabrics or colors that clash—or lack sufficient contrast—with the others. When you have settled on your sequence of fabrics, number them from 1 through 28, beginning with the top of the quilt, as in Diagram 1.

Note: Since there will be no perfectly straight rows of any color on the pieced top, this layout will be a rough approximation of the final appearance of the quilt. Its main purpose is to allow you to number the different fabrics so you'll know how many pieces to cut for each one.

Cutting

First make the templates of the pattern pieces (A, B, C, and D) as shown at the end of this chapter.

Then begin cutting the background/border fabric (see Diagram 2):

2 side borders, 4½″ × 72½″ each (seam allowances *included*)
2 end borders, 4½″ × 48½″ each (seam allowances *included*)
4 squares (template A)
6 large triangles (B)
4 small triangles (C)
8 rectangles (D)

Next, cut the pieces from the 28 fabrics, beginning with fabric 1. Cut each fabric according to the number of pieces specified in Table 1. As soon as you have finished cutting the pieces for a given fabric, be sure to label them with the proper fabric number.

81

Table 1. Cutting Requirements for Hole in the Barn Door	
Fabric	Amount to cut
1, 6, 13, 18, 23, and 28	8 small triangles (template C)
	4 rectangles (D)
2, 7, 12, 17, 22, and 27	7 squares (A)
3, 8, 11, 16, 21, and 26	8 small triangles (C)
	12 rectangles (D)
4, 9, 10, 15, 20, and 25	3 large triangles (B)
	2 small triangles (C)
	6 rectangles (D)
5, 14, 19, and 24	3 large triangles (B)
	2 small triangles (C)
	4 rectangles (D)

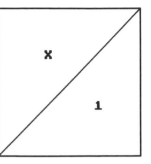

Diagram 4. Piecing End Units for Row A

Scraps No More

Assembling row A

Lay out the pieces for row A—which consists of background fabric (X) and fabric 1—according to Diagram 3, below.

Piece together a small triangle from the background fabric and one from fabric 1 to create a square unit, as in Diagram 4. Make a similar unit for the opposite end of row A. (The only difference between the end units is in the way they are turned when pieced to the rest of the row.)

Next, piece a background rectangle to a fabric 1 rectangle, as in Diagram 5. Make three more such units.

Piece a small fabric 1 triangle to each of the short sides of a large background triangle, as in Diagram 6. Make two more such rectangular units.

Then, following Diagram 3, combine the nine units you've pieced for row A into one long unit. Be sure to place the units so that the background pieces are on top, and piece the unit at the end of each row so that the long side of the background triangle faces the inside of the quilt. When you've finished, label row A and set it aside.

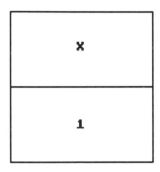

Diagram 5. Piecing Background and Fabric 1 Rectangles

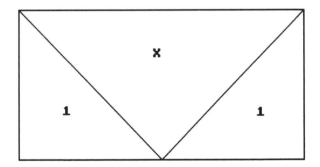

Diagram 6. Piecing Background and Fabric 1 Triangles (Rectangular Unit)

Row B

Row B consists of fabrics 2, 3, and 4 (see Diagram 7, on the facing page). Piece a rectangle from fabric 3 and one from fabric 4 together, joining them on their long sides, as in Diagram 8. Make another such unit for the opposite end of row B.

Diagram 3. Hole in the Barn Door, Row A

Diagram 7. Hole in the Barn Door, Row B

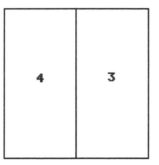

Diagram 8. Piecing End Units for Row B

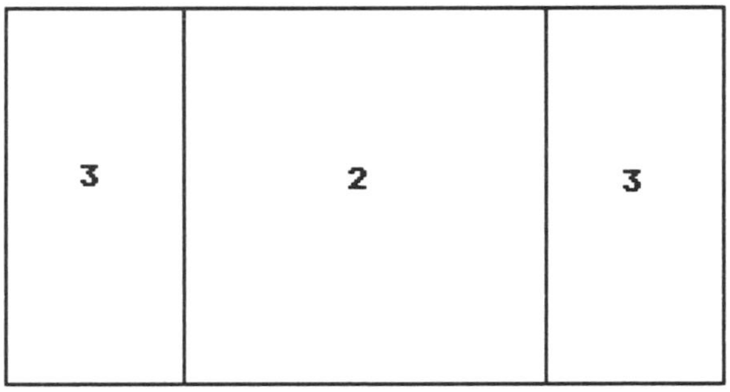

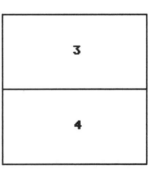

3 and one from fabric 4 to create a square unit, as in Diagram 11. Make a similar unit for the opposite end of row C.

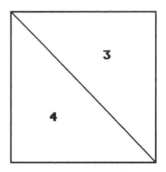

Diagram 11. Piecing End Units for Row C

Piece a fabric 3 and a fabric 4 rectangle together so that the long sides run horizontally, as in Diagram 12. Make three more such units.

Diagram 9. Piecing Rectangular Units for Row B

Piece a fabric 3 rectangle, long side running vertically, to either side of a fabric 2 square, as in Diagram 9. Make two more such rectangular units.

Finally, alternate four fabric 2 squares with these units, adding the end units to complete the row (see Diagram 7, above). Be sure to place each end unit so that the fabric 3 side faces the inside of the quilt. Label row B and set it aside.

Diagram 12. Piecing Rectangles from Fabrics 3 and 4

Then piece a small fabric 3 triangle to each of the short sides of a large fabric 4 triangle, as in Diagram 13, on the following page. Make two more such units.

Row C
Row C consists of fabrics 3 and 4 (see Diagram 10, below). Piece together a small triangle from fabric

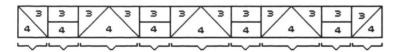

Diagram 10. Hole in the Barn Door, Row C

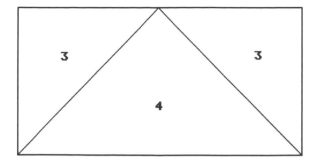

Diagram 13. Piecing Rectangular Units for Row C

Combine the nine units for row C according to Diagram 10. Be sure to place the units so that the fabric 3 pieces are on top, and piece the unit at the end of each row so that the long side of the fabric 3 triangle faces the outside of the quilt. After you've labeled row C, set it aside.

Rows D–R
Continue piecing, referring to Diagram 1 to complete rows D–R. Follow the pattern set in rows A–C, first making the smaller working units (squares and rectangles) required for each row. Each finished row will have nine units: six pieced or intact squares and three pieced rectangle units.

Piece the following rows the same way you did A, but substituting the fabrics indicated for the background and fabric 1:

D—using fabrics 5 and 6
G—using fabrics 10 and 11
J—using fabrics 15 and 16
M—using fabrics 20 and 21
P—using fabrics 25 and 26

Piece these rows the same way you did B, but substituting the fabrics indicated for fabrics 2, 3, and 4:

E—using fabrics 7, 8, and 9
H—using fabrics 10, 11, and 12
K—using fabrics 15, 16, and 17
N—using fabrics 20, 21, and 22
Q—using fabrics 25, 26, and 27

Finally, piece the last rows as you did row C, but substituting the fabrics indicated for fabrics 3 and 4:

F—using fabrics 8 and 9
I—using fabrics 13 and 14
L—using fabrics 18 and 19
O—using fabrics 23 and 24
R—using fabrics 28 and X (the background fabric; note that in piecing the units for this row, you'll place the background units on the *bottom*, which is the opposite of the way the top row is arranged)

When you've pieced each row, arrange rows A through R in order and join them using long crosswise seams.

Assembling the borders
Piece a square on each end of the two end (top and bottom) borders. Set aside.

Add the two side borders to the pieced top; then add the two end borders. This completes the pieced quilt top for Hole in the Barn Door.

Quilting
From the five-yard backing piece, cut two 85″ lengths. Keep one piece intact (about 42″ wide). From the other piece, cut two 9″ widths. Using ¼″ seams, join a 9″ strip to each side of the intact center panel. Press seams toward the outside. Next, place the quilt backing right side down. Smooth the batting over it. Place the pressed quilt top over the batting, right side up. Pin or baste the three layers together for quilting.

Mark quilting lines with a straightedge and soap chip or marking pencil, according to Diagram 14. Quilt along all marked lines using natural-color quilting thread. Mark and quilt the flower motif (Pattern 1) in each corner. Mark and quilt six cable patterns on each side border and four cables on each end border (see Pattern 2).

Finishing
Trim the batting to ½″ larger than the quilt top, to allow for filler in the binding. Trim the quilt backing to match the top. Mark and cut the yard of print fabric you've chosen into 3″-wide bias strips (for a finished binding about ½″ wide). Fold the binding, wrong sides together, and attach it to the quilt front, making sure that the seam goes through all the layers. Turn the binding to the back of the quilt and whipstitch it in place.

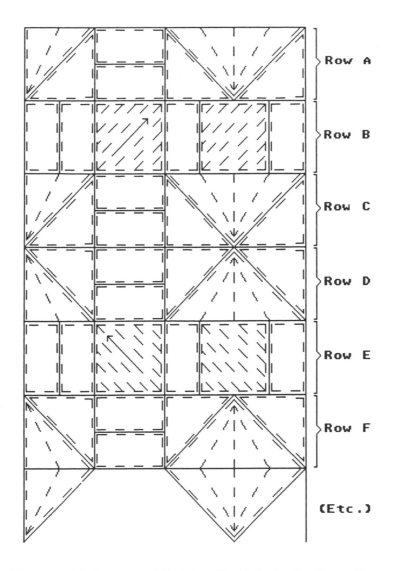

Diagram 14. Suggested Quilting for Hole in the Barn Door

Pattern 1. Flower Motif

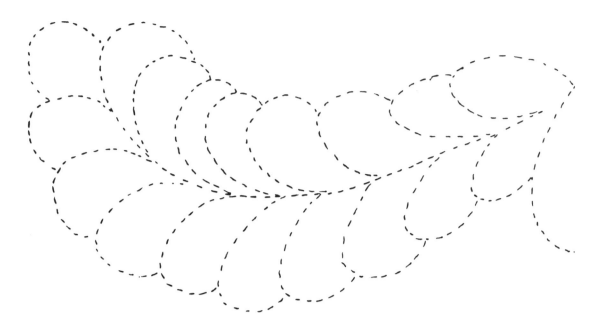

Pattern 2. Cable Motif. Join this half to the one on the facing page to create the full-size cable pattern.

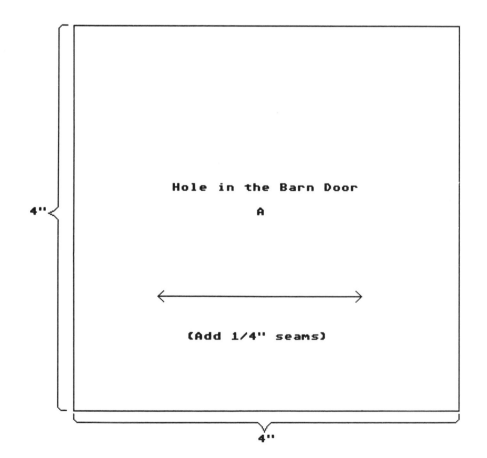

Hole in the Barn Door

A

⟵—————————⟶

(Add 1/4" seams)

4"

4"

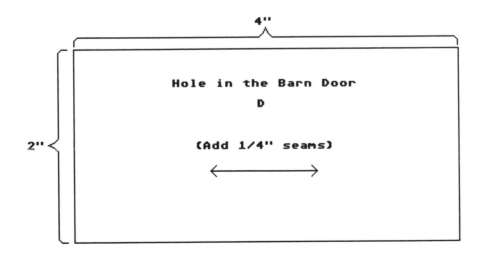

Hole in the Barn Door

D

(Add 1/4" seams)

4"

2"

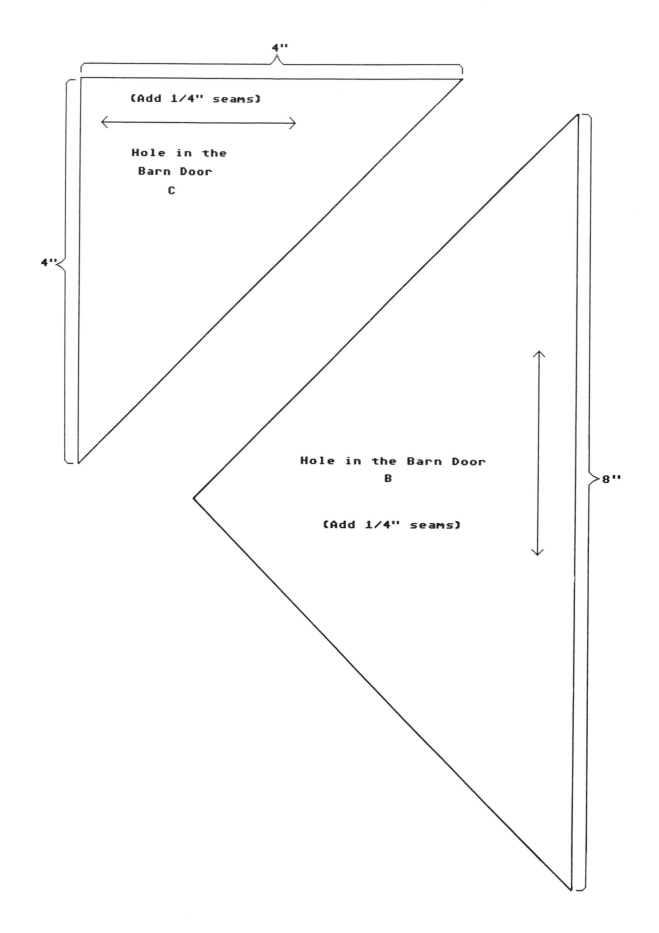

4"

(Add 1/4" seams)

Hole in the
Barn Door
C

4"

Hole in the Barn Door
B

(Add 1/4" seams)

8"

88

12
Escape: A Variation of 'Round the Twist

Quilt by Mary Mousel

For Starters

The following list will help you enjoy a smooth start and steady progress in your work on Escape. It contains a variety of general information about making the quilt.

- **Wash** and **press** all fabrics, including scraps, before you begin.
- For **templates** (patterns of the quilt pieces), use sturdy plastic or sandpaper, and be sure to note grain-line arrows.
- The **cutting and assembly instructions** for Escape are somewhat approximate, since the numbers are in an estimated range. This will produce a design similar, not identical, to that of the pictured quilt.
- The **number of fabrics** to use (and basically, the number of pieces to cut from each) is up to you. This will give you more latitude in designing a quilt based on your special accumulation of fabrics.
- **Seam width** is ¼".
- **Piecing** may be done by machine or hand.

  For **machine** piecing, include the ¼" seam allowances *with* the templates.

  For **hand** piecing, make the templates *without* seam allowances and add them when marking and cutting the fabrics.
- The **finished size** for Escape is 72" × 90".

Supplies

Quilt top fabric
Use 44"/45"-wide cotton or cotton/polyester blends.

Scraps: Select at least five solids in a range of light to dark shades of the same color-family (the colors in the quilt shown include light pink, rose, burgundy, and deep wine). You'll need different amounts for the solids:

light	½ yard
medium light	½ yard
medium	¾ yard
medium dark	¾ yard
dark	2½ yards

In addition, select 10–20 prints in a similar color range—lights, mediums, and darks. Select from fine floral prints, medium prints, bold prints with floral sprays, and border or striped prints. Prints may also include a touch of white, natural, or shades of one other color that complements the solids you've chosen. Select a variety to total about 6 yards.

Minimum scrap size is about 5" × 15". If you're using new fabrics, buy ⅛-yard lengths of each one (which will be enough to cut several pieces from each fabric). For the darker fine prints on the outside of the quilt, you will need about 1 yard each of 3 prints.

Note: Mary used 5 solids and 21 prints in her design. Some prints were used for only one "twist" (the shape—made of four rectangle/triangle combinations—that looks like the broken outline of an octagon). Several prints were used in three twists, while others around the edge of the quilt were used many times. This is why you need such different amounts of each print, and particularly, why you need more of the prints used around the outside.

Backing
Escape requires 5½ yards of good-quality muslin or cotton print for backing.

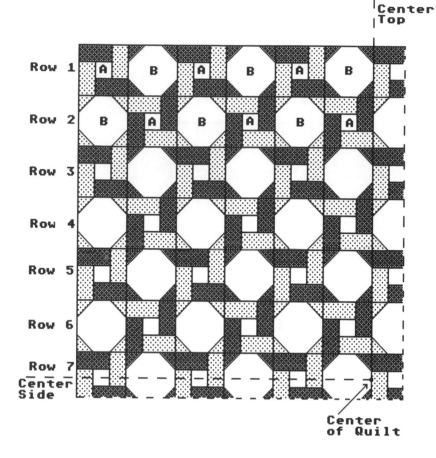

Diagram 1. Detail of Escape Layout: One-Quarter View

Binding
Try the medium-dark solid color you've put in the quilt top (1 yard).

Batting
You'll need 81″ × 96″ of bonded polyester.

Other supplies

iron	2 spools of black quilting
long straightedge	thread
pins	sewing thread
quilting needles	thread for basting
scissors	soap chips or marking pencils
thimble	template material

Optional: Hoop or frame for quilting.

Ready to Work

Cutting
Make templates from the four patterns, Escape 1-4, found at the end of this chapter. As you prepare to cut the fabric pieces, keep in mind that all of the following numbers are approximate.

From the five solid fabrics, cut the number of octagons (E1) indicated:

light	5
medium light	5
medium	15
medium dark	15
dark	50

90

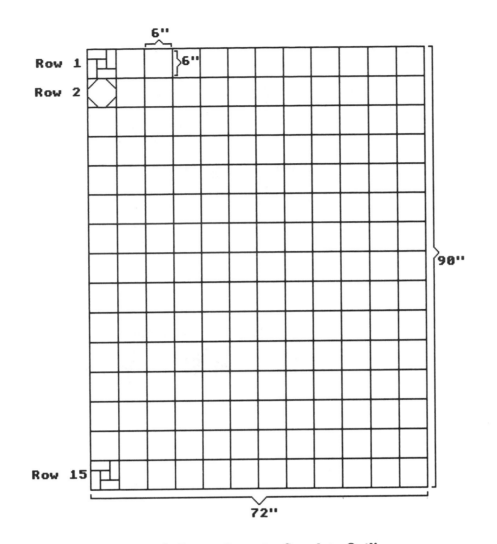

Diagram 2. Escape Layout—Complete Outline

Cut a total of 360 triangles (E2) from the print fabrics. Be sure to note the grain line on the template and faithfully adhere to it. When using border and striped fabrics, always use the *lengthwise* grain only.

Also cut a total of 360 rectangles (E3) from the print fabrics. You need to cut the same number of rectangles and triangles, since those pieces are combined in pairs to form the trapezoid shapes that seem to twist around the octagons and squares. Again, align the grain-line arrow lengthwise for border and striped fabrics.

Finally, cut a total of 90 squares (E4) from the five solid fabrics, following the guidelines given above for cutting out the octagons.

Design suggestions

The success of the Escape design is based on a careful arrangement of light and dark fabrics. A concentration of light octagons at the center of the quilt works its way through darker fabrics to the exterior at the upper right-hand corner of the quilt. The light and medium-light octagons and squares are placed rather freely in the center and toward the upper right, allowing for the "escape" of the quilted butterflies.

The darker solids are concentrated at the perimeter of the quilt, especially at the upper and lower ends. Border and bold-striped print twists are scattered throughout the center—often in sets of three, to avoid too much symmetry and balance.

91

With the use of so many fabrics, it will be necessary for most quiltmakers to lay out their cut pieces before assembly in order to assure good results. In fact, it's helpful to begin by drawing a grid showing your general plan for placing each fabric. Use Diagrams 1–3 as guides. With this general design in mind, begin cutting, adjusting the number of pieces indicated here to suit the design you've planned. As you accumulate cut pieces, arrange them on a large working surface and experiment with possible layouts. Note the interplay of fabrics and shapes, especially the way the trapezoids (rectangle/triangle combinations) twist around the octagons and squares.

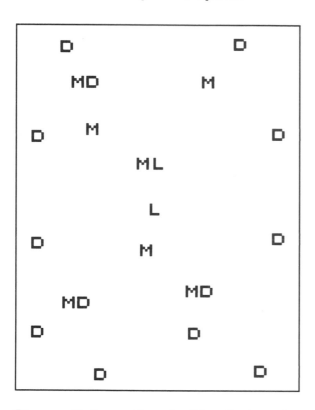

Diagram 3. Suggestions for Distribution of Solid-Colored Fabrics in Escape

  D = *Dark*
 MD = *Medium Dark*
  M = *Medium*
 ML = *Medium Light*
  L = *Light*

Another advantage of laying out the different fabrics before you piece them together is that you can identify the twist portions of the design to be sure that each rectangle/triangle combination matches the others in the twist (see Diagram 1).

When you're using a border or striped print, be certain that border or stripe continues in the same direction across the rectangle to the triangle (see Diagrams 4 and 5). This can be particularly confusing because the rectangle and triangle are not pieced together in the basic units. By first laying out your design, however, you can anticipate where they will meet when the blocks and rows are joined.

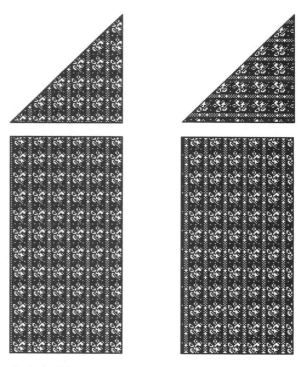

At left: **Diagram 4. Correct Alignment of Rectangle and Triangle to Form Trapezoid**

At right: **Diagram 5. Incorrect Alignment of Rectangle and Triangle**

Scraps No More

Assembly

Escape is composed of two kinds of blocks: unit A and unit B. You will need 90 of each unit to complete the quilt top.

Begin with unit A (see Diagram 6), which is made of one square and four surrounding rectangles. Piece the center square to one of the rectangles (right sides together), sewing down only one-half of the square (and only one-fourth of the rectangle). This partial seam is indicated as number 1 in Diagram 7.

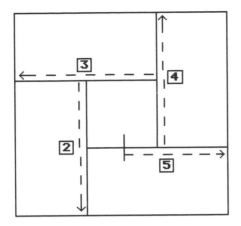

Diagram 6. Escape, Unit A

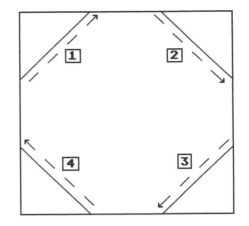

Diagram 8. Escape, Unit B

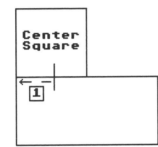

Diagram 7. Piecing First Rectangle to Center of Unit A

Continue adding the other three rectangles in a *clockwise* fashion around the center square. Seams 2–4 are complete, as you see from Diagram 6. The last seam (marked number 5 in the diagram) will be a partial seam to complete the first partial seam.

The completed unit will measure 6″ square. Make 90 such units, referring to your own diagram and layout for proper placement of the rectangles.

To make your first unit B (Diagram 8), find an octagon and the four triangles which correspond to your plan; for instance, if this unit is to be placed beside unit A instead of under it, be sure that its lower left triangle matches the lower right rectangle of unit A. Again, join each piece to the center one, keeping right sides together.

The assembled unit B will also measure 6″ square. Make 90 such units, referring to your own diagram and layout for proper placement of the triangles.

Refer to Diagram 1 for help during the final stages of assembling the quilt top. Begin with the top row (row 1), which consists of 12 blocks (6 of unit A and 6 of unit B). Unit A is the first in this row; piece it to the left-hand side of a B unit. Continue by adding units to the right, alternating A and B, to complete the row. The finished row will measure 72″ × 6″.

To make row 2, begin with a unit B and join it to the left-hand side of an A unit. Add 10 more blocks, alternating B and A, to complete row 2.

Continue piecing rows 3–15. Note that the odd-numbered rows always begin with unit A (on the left) and end with unit B. All even-numbered rows begin with unit B and end with unit A.

Join the 15 rows in long horizontal seams to complete the quilt top.

Quilting
From the 5½-yard backing piece, cut two 95″ lengths. Keep one piece intact (about 42″ wide). From the other piece, cut two 18″ widths; then join a split width to each side of the intact center panel. Press seams toward the outside. After placing the quilt backing right side down, smooth the batting over it. Place the pressed quilt top over the batting, right side up. Pin or baste the three layers together for quilting.

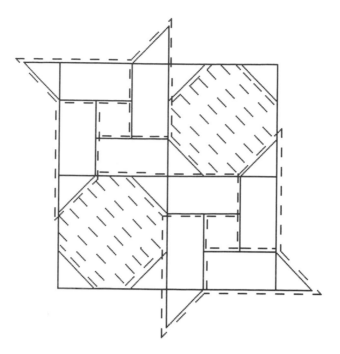

Diagram 9. Quilting Detail for Escape

Mark quilting lines and designs according to Diagram 9 and Patterns 1-4. Mark butterflies on the light, medium/light, medium, and medium/dark octagons. Mark parallel diagonal lines inside the dark octagons, placing them ½″ apart until they fill the octagon, as in Diagram 9.

There are two styles of butterflies; the first has three sizes (Patterns 1-3). Begin by placing the larger sizes near the center of the quilt. As you work toward the outside of the quilt, mark and quilt the smaller size of the first style and several of the second style (Pattern 4).

Quilt "in the ditch," close to the seams around all trapezoids (combined rectangles and triangles), squares, and octagons. Be sure not to quilt along the seam that joins the rectangle with the triangle.

Finishing
Trim the batting to ½″ larger than the quilt top, to allow for filler in the binding. Then trim the quilt backing to match the top. Mark and cut into 3″-wide bias strips the yard of medium-dark fabric you've chosen to complement the solids in the quilt top. Fold the binding, wrong sides together, and attach it to the quilt front; be sure that the seam penetrates all the layers. Turn the binding to the back of the quilt and whipstitch it in place. The finished binding should be about ½″ wide.

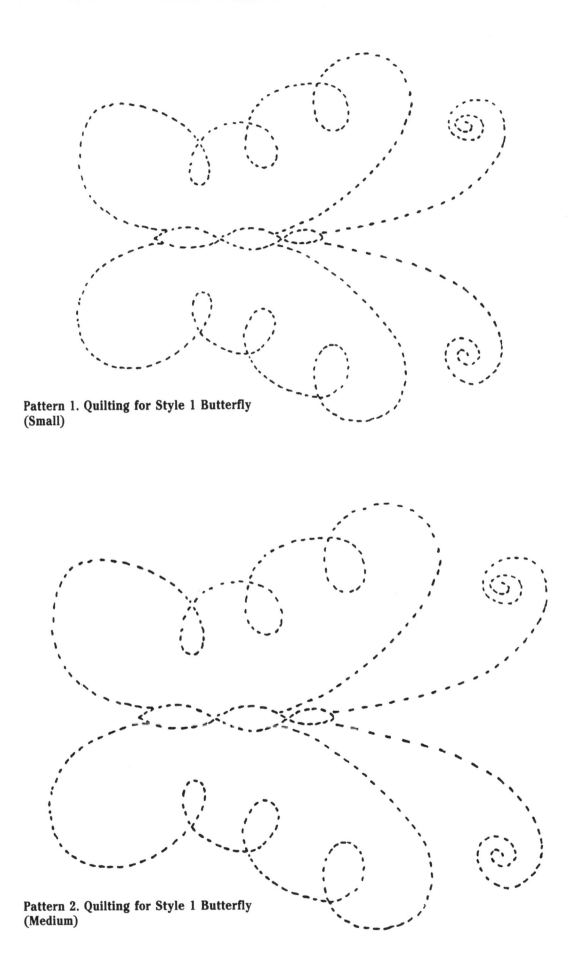

Pattern 1. Quilting for Style 1 Butterfly (Small)

Pattern 2. Quilting for Style 1 Butterfly (Medium)

Pattern 3. Quilting for Style 1 Butterfly (Large)

Pattern 4. Quilting for Style 2 Butterfly

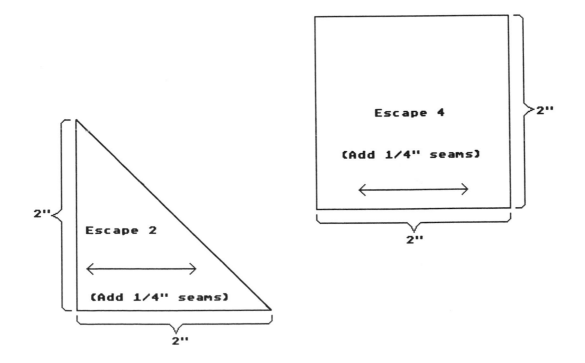

Escape 2

(Add 1/4" seams)

Escape 4

(Add 1/4" seams)

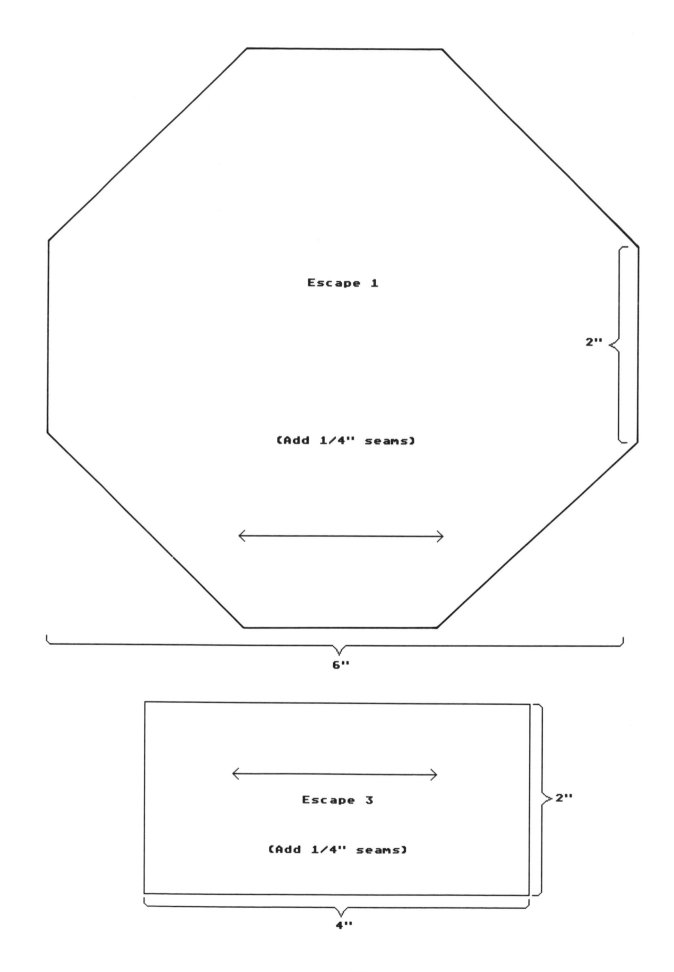

Escape 1

(Add 1/4" seams)

2"

6"

Escape 3

(Add 1/4" seams)

2"

4"

13
Stars and Bars

For Starters

The following list will help you enjoy a smooth start and steady progress in your work on Stars and Bars. It contains a variety of general information about making the quilt.

- **Wash** and **press** all fabrics, including scraps, before you begin.
- For **templates** (patterns of the quilt pieces), use sturdy plastic or sandpaper, and be sure to note grain-line arrows.
- The **units** in Stars and Bars are based on a Star Within a Star (also called Rising Star) design.
- **Seam width** is ¼".
- **Piecing** may be done by machine or hand.

   For **machine** piecing, include the ¼" seam allowances *with* the templates.

   For **hand** piecing, make the templates *without* seam allowances; add them when marking and cutting the fabrics.
- There are **seven units** (each a rectangular "star") in each of the three vertical columns in Stars and Bars.
- The **top and bottom star** on each column is a rectangle measuring 16" × 12", while the other five units each measure 16" × 8".
- The **finished size** for Stars and Bars is 56" × 72".

Supplies

Quilt top fabric
Use 44"/45"-wide cotton or cotton/polyester blends.

Scraps: Use a wide variety of light, medium, and dark scraps in solids, small and medium prints, and fine and bold plaids. To make a quilt like the one pictured, select fabrics from a range of subdued blues, browns, grays, tans, greens, and rusts. I used approximately 150 different fabrics in my design, with 7 fabrics for each star unit. The minimum size required for each center square is about 3" × 3". Larger pieces are needed for background fabrics and the largest stars. The largest piece needed for the corner stars is about 12" × 18".

Borders
The Stars and Bars pictured requires 2¼ yards of a medium blue for its borders.

Binding
You'll need 1 yard of fabric (dark blue was used in the quilt shown).

Backing
This calls for 4½ yards of good-quality unbleached muslin.

Batting
Use 72" × 90" (twin size) bonded polyester.

Other supplies

iron	2 spools of natural-color
long straightedge	quilting thread
pins	sewing thread (a medium
quilting needles	neutral color)
scissors	thread for basting
thimble	soap chips or marking pencils
	template material

Optional: Hoop or frame for quilting.

Ready to Work

Cutting
From the patterns shown at the end of this chapter, make templates labeled SB-1 through SB-10. (*SB* stands for *Stars and Bars.*)

99

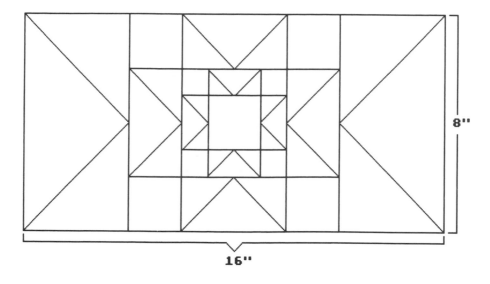

Diagram 1. Stars and Bars, Unit A

Then cut the required number of pieces as listed in Table 1.

Table 1. Cutting Requirements for Stars and Bars

Template	Number of Pieces to Cut
SB-1	21 (1 from each fabric)
SB-2	168 (8 each from 21 fabrics)
SB-3	84 (4 each from 21 fabrics)
SB-4	84 (4 each from 21 fabrics)
SB-5	168 (8 each from 21 fabrics)
SB-6	84 (4 each from 21 fabrics)
SB-7	84 (4 each from 21 fabrics)
SB-8	96 (4 each from 15 fabrics; 6 each from 6 fabrics)
SB-9	48 (2 each from 15 fabrics; 3 each from 6 fabrics)
SB-10	12 (2 each from 6 fabrics)
	849 (total pieces)

From the 2¼ yards of medium-blue fabric, cut 2 side borders, 4½″ × 72½″ each (allowances for seams and mitering *included*), and cut 2 end borders, 4½″ × 56½ each (again, seam and mitering allowances included).

Scraps No More

Note on fabric placement: Before you begin piecing the individual units, plan the fabric combination that you want to use for each. Think of the quilt design as 21 incomplete stars. Gather your scraps in groups of 7 compatible fabrics (one group for each star), including both lights and darks. In each group, include at least one stripe or plaid, and select one fabric for the center square. Then build the star rectangle outward, laying out a light fabric, then a dark, and so on, alternating until you reach the seventh (dark) fabric.

Assembly of units

There are two construction units, A and B (Diagrams 1 and 8). Beginning with unit A, gather the 39 pieces needed for a single unit. Join the long side of the smallest triangle, SB-2, to a shorter side of the triangle SB-3, as in Diagram 2. Add another SB-2 to the opposite side, as in Diagram 3, to form a rectangular unit. Make three more of these units. Set two aside. Join the other two to opposite sides of the center square, SB-1, as in Diagram 4, to complete the center unit of the star.

100

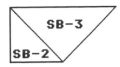

Diagram 2. Piecing SB-2 to SB-3

Diagram 3. Completing the First Rectangular Unit

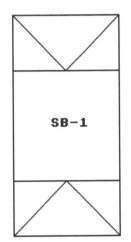

Diagram 4. Piecing Center Unit of Smallest Star

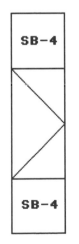

Diagram 5. Piecing Side Unit of Smallest Star

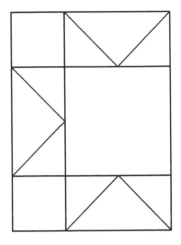

Diagram 6. Joining Side Unit of Star to Center Unit

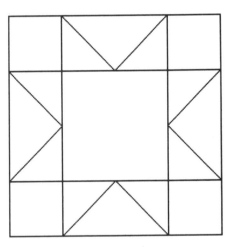

Diagram 7. Complete Star Unit

Add a small square (SB-4) to the top and one to the bottom of each of the two units that were set aside (see Diagram 5). Join these new units to opposite sides of the center square (Diagram 6) to complete the smallest star (Diagram 7). This unit will be the center square for the next, medium-sized star.

To begin the next star, join the long side of the SB-5 triangle to a shorter side of SB-6. Add another SB-5 to the opposite side (this is the same process as in Diagrams 2 and 3, except that the pieces are larger). Make three more of these units. Join one of them to the top and the other to the bottom of the small star unit completed earlier (a process parallel to the one illustrated in Diagram 4).

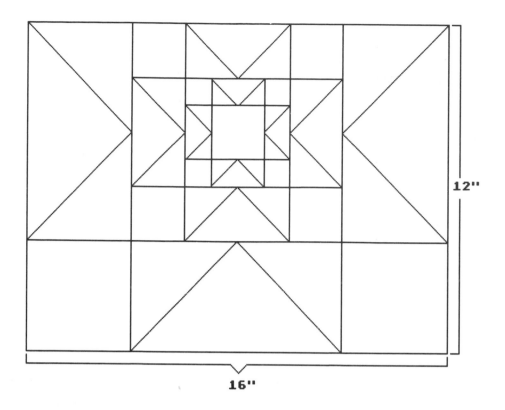

12"

16"

Diagram 8. Stars and Bars, Unit B

Add an SB-7 square to the top and one to the bottom of each of the other SB-5/SB-6 units. (Proportionately, this looks the same as Diagram 5.) Join the resulting units to opposite sides of the small star unit, and this completes the medium-sized star. Keep in mind that the smallest (4") stars and the medium-sized (8") stars are complete in design, forming eight points, while the two larger stars only have four (or six) points.

Continue piecing to form the larger, incomplete star. Attach the long side of an SB-8 triangle to a shorter side of SB-9; then add another SB-8 to the opposite side. Join this unit, lengthwise, to the left side of the medium-sized star, making sure that the large triangle points toward the center of the star. Make another SB-8/SB-9 unit and join it to the right side of the star, again with the large triangle pointing toward the center of the star. This completes unit A (Diagram 1). Make 14 more of these smaller rectangular units.

To make unit B, gather all the required pieces (44) according to Diagram 8. Piece the unit just as you pieced unit A; the only additional step is to add a rectangular unit consisting of two SB-8's,

one SB-9, and two SB-10's to either the top or bottom of the A unit. Make the extra rectangle by piecing each SB-8 to a shorter side of the SB-9 triangle. Then add an SB-10 to each end of this unit, as in the bottom part of Diagram 8, and piece the new section to the base (the part that's identical to unit A). This completes unit B. Make five more of these larger rectangular units.

Design suggestions

After you have completed all the A and B units, set them aside for a while. At a later time—when your mind is fresh and free from the fatigue of working with 150 fabrics, lay out all the units on a large working area.

Arrange the units in three vertical columns. Rearrange the units, looking for effective interplay of lights and darks and color mixtures. Stand back at a distance to get the overall impact of the fabric mixtures. Keep rearranging until you determine a design layout that pleases you. Don't be in a hurry.

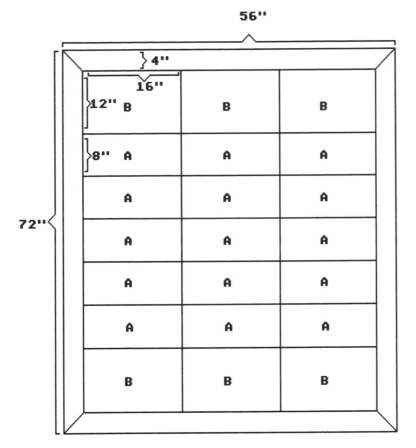

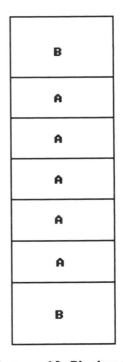

Diagram 9. Stars and Bars Layout

Diagram 10. Piecing the
Columns for Stars
and Bars

Assembly of quilt top

Diagram 9 indicates the layout of the quilt top. Begin with the left column. Piece five of the A units together (as pictured in Diagram 10); then add one of the B units to the top and one to the bottom of the column. Piece the middle and right columns in the same manner.

Join the three columns in two lengthwise seams, taking care to see that all of the star points meet and match.

Finally, add the four borders, mitering the corners. This completes the quilt top as shown in Diagram 9.

Quilting

From the 4½ yards of muslin, cut two 80″ lengths. Keep one intact (about 42″ wide), and from the other piece, cut two 15″ widths. Join a split width to each side of the intact center panel. Press seams toward the outside.

Place quilt backing right side down. Smooth the batting over it. Place the pressed quilt top over the batting, right side up. Pin or baste the three layers together for quilting.

Mark quilting lines according to Diagram 11, with a soap chip and straightedge. Quilt along all marked lines.

Finishing

Trim the batting to ½″ larger than the quilt top, to allow for filler in the binding. Trim the quilt backing to match the top. From the yard of dark-blue fabric, mark and cut 3″-wide bias strips (for a finished binding about ½″ wide). Fold the binding, wrong sides together. Then attach it to the quilt front in a seam that penetrates all the layers. Turn the binding to the back of the quilt and whipstitch it into place.

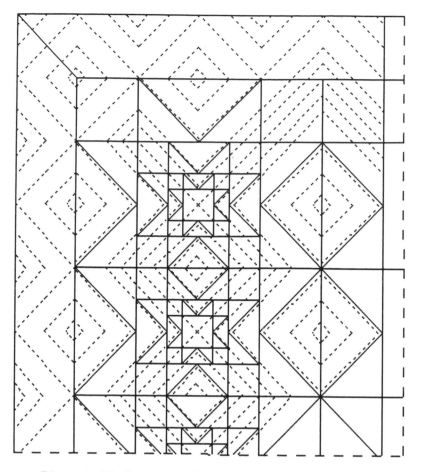

Diagram 11. Suggested Quilting for Stars and Bars

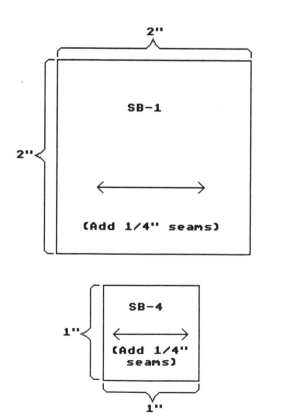

SB-1

2"

2"

(Add 1/4" seams)

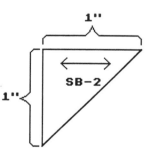

1"

1"

SB-2

(Add 1/4" seams)

SB-4

1"

1"

(Add 1/4" seams)

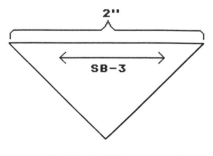

2"

SB-3

(Add 1/4" seams)

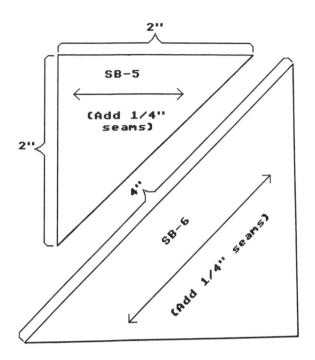

2"

SB-5

(Add 1/4"
seams)

2"

4"

SB-6

(Add 1/4" seams)

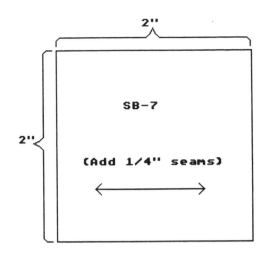

2"

SB-7

2"

(Add 1/4" seams)

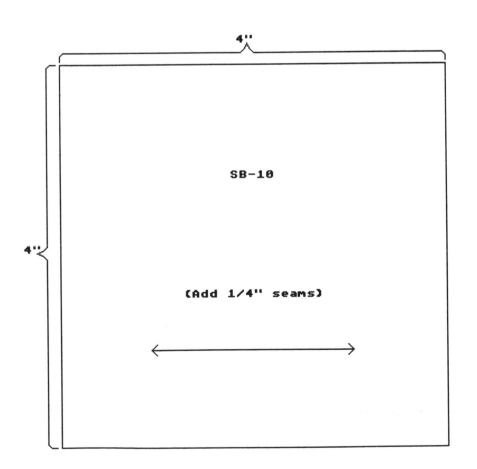

4"

SB-10

4"

(Add 1/4" seams)

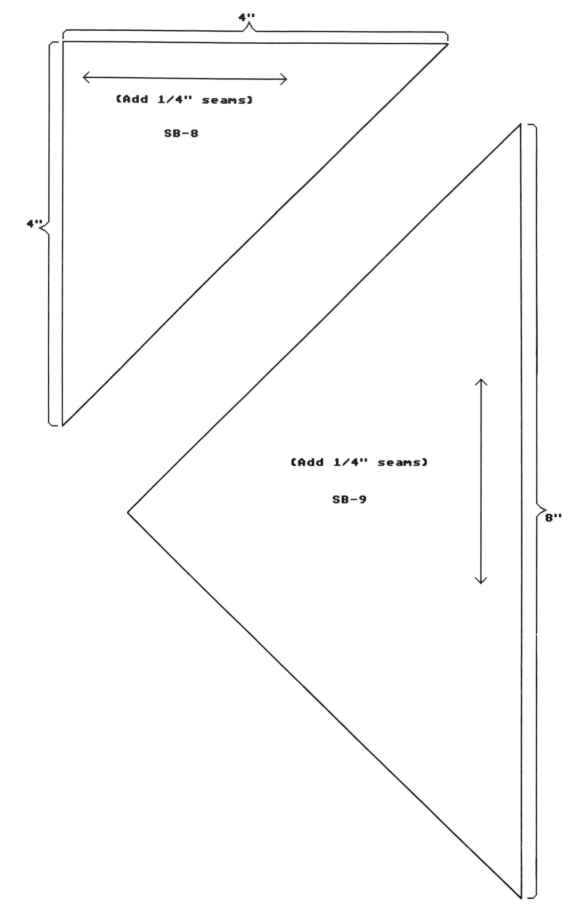

4"

(Add 1/4" seams)

SB-8

4"

(Add 1/4" seams)

SB-9

8"

106

Bibliography

For Techniques and Patterns

American Patchwork & Quilting. Des Moines: Meredith Corporation, 1985.

Beyer, Jinny. *The Scrap Look (Designs, Fabrics, Colors, and Piecing Techniques for Creating Multi-Fabric Quilts)*. McLean, Virginia: EPM Publications, Inc., 1985.

Florence, Judy. *Award-Winning Quilts and How to Make Them*. Radnor, Pennsylvania: Wallace-Homestead Book Company, 1986.

_____. *Award-Winning Quilts, Book II*. Radnor, Pennsylvania. Wallace-Homestead Book Company, 1986.

_____. *Award-Winning Quick Quilts*. Radnor, Pennsylvania: Wallace-Homestead Book Company, 1988.

_____. *A Collection of Favorite Quilts: Narratives, Directions, and Patterns for 15 Quilts*. Paducah, Kentucky: American Quilter's Society, 1990.

_____. *More Projects & Patterns: A Second Collection of Favorite Quilts*. Paducah, Kentucky: American Quilter's Society, 1992.

Halgrimson, Jan. *Great Scrap-Bag Quilts*. Edmonds, Washington: Weaver-Finch Publications, 1980.

_____. *Scraps Can Be Beautiful*. Edmonds, Washington: Weaver-Finch Publications, 1979.

Horton, Roberta. *Calico and Beyond: The Use of Patterned Fabric in Quilts*. Lafayette, California: C & T Publishing, 1986.

_____. *Plaids & Stripes: The Use of Directional Fabric in Quilts*. Lafayette, California: C&T Publishing, 1990.

Martin, Judy. *Scrap Quilts*. Wheatridge, Colorado: Moon over the Mountain Publishing Company, 1985.

Quilting, Patchwork & Appliqué. Menlo Park, California: Lane Publishing Company, 1982.

Walker, Michele. *The Complete Book of Quiltmaking*. New York: Alfred A. Knopf, 1986.

For Inspiration and Ideas

Bishop, Robert. *New Discoveries in American Quilts*. New York: E. P. Dutton & Company, Inc., 1975.

Holstein, Jonathan. *The Pieced Quilt: An American Design Tradition*. Boston: New York Graphic Society, 1973.

Lipsett, Linda. *Remember Me (Women & Their Friendship Quilts)*. San Francisco: The Quilt Digest Press, 1985.

Nelson, Cyril I. *The Quilt Engagement Calendar*. New York: E. P. Dutton, 1977 to date.

Packer, Barbara, ed. *The State of the Art Quilt: Contemporary Quilts for the Collector*. East Meadow, New York: Friends of Nassau County Recreation, 1985.

Pellman, Rachel and Kenneth. *Amish Crib Quilts*. Intercourse, Pennsylvania: Good Books, 1985.

_____. *The World of Amish Quilts*. Intercourse, Pennsylvania: Good Books, 1984.

The Quilt Digest. Volumes 1, 2, 3, and 4. San Francisco: The Quilt Digest Press, 1983–1986.

Tomlonson, Judy Schroeder. *Mennonite Quilts and Pieces*. Intercourse, Pennsylvania: Good Books, 1985.

Williamson, Darra Duffy. *Sensational Scrap Quilts*. Paducah, Kentucky: American Quilter's Society, 1992.